PRACTICAL
GOURMET
Companion
to

Superfood Juicing and Smoothies

Wendy Pirk • Tamara Eder • James Darcy

Library and Archives Canada Cataloguing in Publication
Pirk, Wendy, 1973-, author
        Superfood juicing and smoothies / Wendy Pirk, Tamara
Eder, James Darcy.

(Original series)
Includes index.
ISBN 978-1-988133-07-2 (wire-o)

        1. Fruit juices. 2. Vegetable juices. 3. Smoothies
(Beverages). 4. Cooking (Natural foods). 5. Cookbooks I. Eder,
Tamara, 1974-, author II. Darcy, James, author III. Title.

TX840.J84P57 2016   641.87'5   C2016-901695-1

Distributed by
Canada Book Distributors - Booklogic
11414-119 Street
Edmonton. Alberta, Canada T5G 2X6
Tel: 1-800-661-9017

We acknowledge the financial support of the Government of Canada through the Canada
Book Fund for our publishing activities.

Funded by the Government of Canada | Canadä
Financé par le gouvernement du Canada

PC: 28

TABLE OF CONTENTS

Practical Gourmet

Practical Gourmet is delighted to partner with Company's Coming to introduce a new series designed to help home cooks create no-fuss, sumptuous food. Titles in this series feature step-by-step instructions, full-page colour photos with every recipe and sidebars on preparation tips and tricks.

We are excited to bring you *Superfood Juicing and Smoothies,* the newest title in this series. In this busy age when downtime seems to be a luxury for many of us, it is easy to turn to prepackaged convenient foods rather than preparing healthy meals at home. These prepackaged foods, however, can take a huge toll on your health, not to mention your pocketbook. Fortunately, in this book, we have a solution. Smoothies and juicing are easy ways to bring nutritious food back into the equation in a quick and convenient manner.

With their focus on natural whole foods, the recipes in this book deliver juices and smoothies that are simple and convenient to prepare but are sophisticated enough in flavour to please even the most gourmet palate. Occasionally we go beyond the common ingredients and throw in a few you might not be so familiar with, but that deserve a place in your diet. So power up your juicer or blender and enjoy.

The Jean Paré Story

Jean Paré (pronounced "jeen PAIR-ee") grew up understanding that the combination of family, friends and home cooking is the best recipe for a good life. When Jean left home, she took with her a love of cooking, many family recipes and an intriguing desire to read cookbooks as if they were novels!

When her four children had all reached school age, Jean volunteered to cater the 50th anniversary celebration of the Vermilion School of Agriculture, now Lakeland College, in Alberta, Canada. Working out of her home, Jean prepared a dinner for more than 1,000 people, launching a flourishing catering operation that continued for over 18 years.

As requests for her recipes increased, Jean was often asked the question, "Why don't you write a cookbook?" The publication of *150 Delicious Squares* on April 14, 1981 marked the debut of what would soon become one of the world's most popular cookbook series.

"Never share a recipe you wouldn't use yourself."

Company's Coming cookbooks are distributed in Canada, the United States, Australia and other world markets. Bestsellers many times over in English, Company's Coming cookbooks have also been published in French and Spanish.

Familiar and trusted in home kitchens around the world, Company's Coming cookbooks are offered in a variety of formats. Highly regarded as kitchen workbooks, the softcover Original Series, with its lay-flat plastic comb binding, is still a favourite among readers.

Jean Paré's approach to cooking has always called for quick and easy recipes using everyday ingredients. That view has served her well.

Jean continues to share what she calls The Golden Rule of Cooking: Never share a recipe you wouldn't use yourself. It's an approach that has worked—millions of times over!

Introduction

There is no official definition of what a superfood is. The term is often overused, or misused to sell food products or supplements that have unsubstantiated health benefits, or that have been exaggerated to the status of miracle foods. Although there are obviously no miracle foods, there are some foods that are especially nutrient-dense, and that offer additional health benefits beyond simple nutrition. These are what we are calling superfoods. Essentially, superfoods are foods that give you more "bang for your buck," nutritionally speaking. They contain high levels of some or all of the following, all of which are necessary for good health: antioxidants, healthy fats, fibre, phytochemicals, minerals and vitamins.

Berries, for example, are often given superfood status, not only because they are packed with vitamins, minerals and fibre, but because of their high levels of antioxidants. In particular, berries are high in one group of antioxidants called flavonoids that are thought to be especially powerful.

Some of the benefits flavonoids have been credited with include repairing DNA damage, reducing inflammation, making cancer cells more receptive to chemotherapeutic drugs, and combating the toxic effects of cancer treatment. Anthocyanins, a type of flavonoid found in blueberries, can help prevent macular degeneration, improve memory and general cognitive function and may even offer protection from Alzheimer's. Ellagic acid, found in raspberries and blackberries, is another type of antioxidant and is thought to prevent the growth of tumours and help the liver remove carcinogens from the blood.

The list of superfoods is always under flux as researchers make new discoveries in the field of food science, but most are "whole foods," meaning you would traditionally find them in a garden or the produce aisle at the supermarket. Many well-known, favourite foods may easily be elevated to superfood status if research discovers that they have a particular health benefit.

It is important to note that eating superfoods will not "fix" unhealthy lifestyle choices; you can't expect to avoid lung cancer by eating berries if you are a smoker, and adding a variety of superfoods to a diet that is high in poor nutritional choices, such as processed foods and refined sugars, will not make you healthy. However, for those who are already eating a healthy, well-balanced diet, superfoods are an extra nutritional boost that can keep you feeling great and help keep chronic disease at bay.

Essential Vitamins and Minerals for Good Health

The body needs both vitamins and minerals to grow and function properly. These nutrients are not produced in the body (except vitamin D) and instead must come from the food that we eat. Vitamin and mineral deficiencies prevent the body from working as well as it should and can have an enormous effect on overall health, possibly resulting in illness, chronic disease or even death.

Vitamins fall into two categories: fat-soluble and water-soluble. Fat-soluble vitamins are stored in fatty tissue in the body and are absorbed more easily when they are consumed with a source of dietary fat. Because they can accumulate in the body, you should not exceed the recommended daily intake for these vitamins or you can harm your health. Fat-soluble vitamins include vitamins A, D, E and K. Water-soluble vitamins, which include the B vitamins and vitamin C, are not stored in the body; instead, what the body doesn't use gets flushed out in urine. The only exception is vitamin B12, which can be stored in the liver for several years.

FAT-SOLUBLE VITAMINS

Vitamin A: this group of nutrients is essential for healthy vision and for normal cell growth. It also helps support the immune system and proper organ function, including the heart, kidneys and lungs. Vitamin A can be found in leafy greens, dark-coloured fruit, egg yolks, liver, beef, fish and fortified dairy products.

Vitamin D: also called the sunshine vitamin, vitamin D helps the body absorb calcium and maintains proper levels of calcium and phosphorus in the blood. It also helps the immune system fight off viruses, and nerves need vitamin D to send messages between different parts of the body and the brain. Vitamin D is produced in the body when skin is exposed to the sun, but many people do not get enough sun exposure to meet the recommended daily intake of this vitamin. Vitamin D does not occur naturally in many foods but can be found in fortified milk products and cereals as well as in fatty fish like salmon and cod liver oil.

Vitamin E: there are eight nutrients in this group of vitamins, and all are antioxidants, which help prevent oxidative stress in the cells. Vitamin E is also important for the formation of red blood cells and helps the body use vitamin K. Good sources of vitamin E include avocado, dark green vegetables like spinach, asparagus and broccoli, corn and safflower oil, papaya, mango, wheat germ, seeds and nuts.

Vitamin K: this group of vitamins is essential for blood clotting and also helps regulate the amount of calcium in the blood. Vitamin K can be found in cabbage, cauliflower and dark leafy greens such as spinach, Swiss chard and kale, as well as fish, eggs and beef.

WATER-SOLUBLE VITAMINS

B vitamins: as a whole, this group of vitamins is necessary for the body to convert food into energy, but each type within this group also has its own function.

B1: also called thiamine, this vitamin helps the body change carbohydrates into energy and supports the nervous system. It can be found in eggs, organ meats, legumes, nuts, seeds and whole grains

B2: known as riboflavin, this B vitamin also helps convert food into energy and is essential for the production of red blood cells. It also helps maintain proper vision. B2 can be found in eggs, dairy products, leafy greens, legumes and nuts.

B3: otherwise known as niacin, this vitamin can help lower cholesterol, support the cardiovascular system and is important for maintaining healthy skin and nerves. Good sources of niacin include avocado, eggs, fortified cereals and bread products, legumes, nuts, potatoes, tuna and poultry.

B5: usually called pantothenic acid, this vitamin is especially important for metabolizing food and also plays a role in hormone production. It can be found in avocado, the brassica family of vegetables, legumes, mushrooms, whole grain cereals, potatoes and sweet potatoes, as well as eggs, organ meats and milk.

B6: also called pyridoxine, B6 helps in the formation of red blood cells and supports the immune system and brain function. It can be found in avocado, bananas, legumes, nuts and meat.

B7: not much is known about this B vitamin, also called biotin, but it helps the body metabolize protein and carbohydrates, and it may help in processing glucose. Biotin is also important for healthy skin and nails. It can be found in egg yolks, legumes, milk products, organ meats and nuts.

B9: also called folate, B9 is essential for DNA and RNA production as well as proper brain function. It also works with B12 to form red blood cells. Folate can be found in asparagus, broccoli, beets, legumes, leafy greens, oranges, peanut butter and wheat germ. Its synthetic form, folic acid, is often added to fortified cereals.

B12: this vitamin supports the central nervous system and works with B9 to form red blood cells. It can only be found in animal products including meat, dairy products and eggs. Some breakfast cereals are fortified with B12.

Vitamin C: also called ascorbic acid, vitamin C is a powerful antioxidant. It also helps the body heal wounds, aids in iron absorption and is essential for healthy teeth and gums. Good sources of vitamin C include broccoli, potatoes, citrus fruits, berries and tomatoes.

MINERALS

The body needs certain minerals to be healthy and strong, and these minerals are found only in the soil. Plants absorb these minerals as they grow, and we in turn absorb the minerals from the plants that we eat, or from the meat of animals that have fed on the plants. Some of the essential minerals necessary for good health, and the foods that contain these minerals, are listed below.

Calcium: this mineral is best known for building and maintaining strong bones and teeth, but it is also necessary for proper metabolic function, including muscle contractions and blood clotting. Calcium is stored in bones and teeth; if your diet is deficient in calcium, your body will leach the calcium it needs from these stores, undermining their strength and potentially leading to low bone mass or osteoporosis. The body loses calcium through sweat and urination, and diets high in sodium can increase the amount of calcium that is lost. Good sources of calcium include dairy products, almonds, dates, kelp, sesame seeds and molasses.

Iron: essential for carrying oxygen in the blood to tissue, iron plays an important role in keeping the body energized. Iron deficiency can lead to anemia, which is characterized by weakness and fatigue. There are two types of iron—heme and non-heme. Heme iron comes from meat, fish, seafood and poultry; non-heme comes from plant sources such as spinach, whole grains, kale, almonds, broccoli and dried legumes. Non-heme iron is not absorbed by the body as well as heme iron, but combining non-heme iron sources with vitamin C can help with absorption.

Magnesium: the body uses magnesium to convert food to energy, and it is also essential for proper nerve function. Magnesium also works with calcium to build and maintain strong bones; deficiency can lead to metabolic syndrome, heart disease and osteoporsis. Signs of deficiency include muscle cramps, facial ticks and chronic pain. Dietary sources of magnesium include nuts and seeds, legumes, whole grains and dark green vegetables.

Manganese: because it helps with the absorption of calcium, manganese is essential for proper bone development; it is also necessary for proper blood clotting, and brain and nerve functioning. Manganese also helps with metabolizing fat and carbohydrates as well as regulating blood sugar, and it has antioxidant function, fighting free radicals that can cause disease. Evidence suggests that this mineral can also help relieve the symptoms of PMS. Deficiency can lead to osteoporosis and has been linked with seizures and general weakness. Good sources of manganese include whole grains, nuts and seeds, legumes and pineapple.

Phosphorus: necessary for strong bones and teeth, phosphorus also helps with energy production. It can be found in almost all fruits and vegetables.

Potassium: along with sodium, potassium works to regulate the amount of water the body retains. It also supports heart health, bolsters the immune system, helps muscles and nerves function properly and assists with nutrient absorption. Deficiency may lead to low blood pressure, irritability and cellulite formation. Potassium can be found in bananas, almonds, legumes, celery, potatoes, papaya, pumpkin (including the seeds) and leafy greens such as spinach and Swiss chard.

Selenium: the body needs very little of this mineral, but it works with various other nutrients, including vitamins C and E, to protect cells and DNA from being damaged by free radicals. Selenium can be found in asparagus, bananas, coconut, guava, mango, pomegranate and legumes.

Zinc: this mineral helps heal tissue, supports both the nervous system and the immune system and helps to regulate hormones. It can be found in nuts, oats, sesame seeds, legumes and pumpkin (including the seeds), as well as seafood and lamb.

Other Beneficial Phytonutrients

Broadly speaking, a phytonutrient is any substance that originates in plants that nourishes the body and is essential for growth or for maintaining life. Vitamins and minerals are obvious phytonutrients, but there are other substances that are essential to good health that do not fit in those two categories.

Antioxidants: although we need oxygen to live, in the form of free radicals, oxygen attacks cells in the body, creating oxidative stress. Free radicals are unstable oxygen molecules that steal electrons from healthy cells, causing them to weaken, mutate or die. As more cells become damaged, the body becomes susceptible to illness and degenerative diseases. Antioxidants are like molecular superheroes, thwarting free radicals and preventing them from causing harm by "donating" one of their electrons to the free radical, thereby neutralizing it and the threat is poses to surrounding cells.

Chlorophyll: the same pigment that gives plants their vibrant green colour, chlorophyll also provides a number of health benefits for the human body. Foremost, chlorophyll is a natural blood purifier; it removes any detritus left behind by the immune system as it fights foreign bodies in the blood, reducing the possibility of cell damage. Chlorophyll also has anti-inflammatory and antioxidant properties, and it keeps the body's pH in balance. For optimum health, the body should be slightly alkaline, but the typical North American diet is high in acid-forming foods, which then throws off the body's pH balance. A body that is out of balance is more susceptible to infection and disease.

Enzymes: although the body produces enzymes, it also benefits from enzymes produced by plants and animals. Enzymes are proteins that act as catalysts, triggering chemical reactions in the body that are necessary for proper functioning and growth. They can help with digestion and the absorption of nutrients, as well as supporting the processes that are necessary for tissue growth and reproduction, to name a few. Enzymes are destroyed by heat, so smoothies are the perfect way to get these chemicals into your diet.

Fibre: perhaps best known for its role in relieving constipation, fibre is an essential nutrient that most North Americans do not get enough of. Fibre helps eliminate waste and toxins from the body, supports heart health, helps regulate blood sugar and can play a role in maintaining a healthy body weight. There are two types of fibre: soluble and insoluble. Soluble fibre binds with water to push waste and toxins through the digestive tract. Insoluble fibre does not dissolve and so adds bulk to stool, helping to promote regularity and maintain a healthy digestive system.

Protein: often called the building blocks of life, protein is in every cell of your body, from your bones and cartilage to your tissues to your hair. In fact, hair and nails are built almost entirely from protein. The body needs protein to build, maintain and repair cells, and it is also important for the production of hormones and enzymes that perform various functions throughout the body. Protein is made up of essential and nonessential amino acids. Nonessential amino acids are those the body can produce itself, but essential amino acids must be obtained through an outside source, namely food or supplements. A complete protein is one that contains all the essential amino acids. Most complete proteins are from animal sources, such as meat or dairy products, but there are a few plant sources of complete protein as well. Chia seeds, hemp seeds and quinoa are the three sources included in this book.

Why Smoothies?

There is no easier way to boost the nutrition in your diet than by incorporating smoothies. To be clear, we are not talking about the sugar-laden, milkshake wannabes of dubious nutritional value that have made their way onto the menus of fast-food chains and smoothie shops across the nation. We are talking about nutrient-rich smoothies made with natural whole foods that nourish the body and support good health.

Quick and convenient, smoothies are an obvious choice for today's busy lifestyle, whether you are looking for a healthy snack between meals or the meal itself. You might not have time in the morning to cook a healthy breakfast before heading out the door, but you can most likely squeeze in the 2 minutes or so that it takes to whip up a smoothie. And because it's portable, you can happily sip away as you navigate your way to where you need to be.

Another bonus is that research has shown that blending foods not only makes them easier to digest, but also makes the nutrients they contain more bioavailable. In other words, once the blades have pulverized the ingredients into smoothie goodness, the body has an easier time absorbing the nutrients the ingredients contain.

Perhaps the best feature of smoothies, though, is their versatility. Eating the same old salad everyday to get your greens can get a little old, but toss a few handfuls of said greens into your fruit smoothie and you are getting all of their nutritional benefits while barely noticing they are there. The same can be said for a variety of ingredients. Vegetables, fruits, nuts, seeds, grains and even legumes can be blended into a filling drink that in the end tastes more like a dessert than a healthy meal. Smoothies are also a great way to experiment with new ways to use your favourite veggies. Who knew sweet potato would make for a fantastic smoothie? Trust us, it does.

In the recipes in this book, we've focused more on whole foods, meaning that whenever possible we've chosen fruit instead of fruit juice, or a naturally high-protein ingredient such as hemp or chia instead of manufactured protein powders. In the interest of keeping these smoothies healthful, we've also avoided adding refined sugar, preferring to rely on the natural sweetness of the ingredients instead, and adding in a more natural sweetener when necessary. Use the recipes provided as they are, or build on them to give them your own flair.

As you experiment with ingredients and tweak recipes to fit your preferences, don't expect that every combination is going to be a winner. Should you have a smoothie disaster (yup, they happen, even to seasoned smoothie makers) and the end result is unpalatable, all is not lost. Instead of pouring it down the drain, freeze the offending smoothie in ice cube trays and then add an ice cube or two to the next few smoothies you make until all the ice cubes have been used. You'll still benefit from the nutrients in the foul-tasting smoothie, but the fruits and veggies in the fresh smoothie will mask the unpleasant flavour of smoothie-gone-wrong.

Summer Breeze

Is there any greater pleasure on a hot summer's day than lounging on a deck or patio with a cool breeze in your hair, sipping on a frosty, fruity smoothie? Tart raspberries pair perfectly with sweet, juicy peaches to provide large doses niacin, potassium and vitamins, including vitamins A and C. Almonds are loaded with antioxidants, many of which are found in the brown skin, so choose raw nuts over blanched. Sunflower seeds are also antioxidant powerhouses and are high in vitamin E and folic acid, as well as calcium and iron. We've used frozen raspberries in this recipe because they make the smoothie frostier, but you could use fresh raspberries if you have some on hand.

Frozen raspberries	1 cup	250 mL
Chopped fresh peaches	1 cup	250 mL
Almonds	1/4 cup	60 mL
Sunflower seed butter	1 tbsp.	15 mL
Coconut water	1 cup	250 mL

Combine all the ingredients in a blender until smooth. Makes 2 servings.

1 serving: 200 Calories; 7 g Total Fat (2 g Mono, 1 g Poly, 0.5 g Sat); 0 mg Cholesterol; 33 g Carbohydrate (8 g Fibre, 23 g Sugar); 5 g Protein; 125 mg Sodium

When making smoothies, choose freestone peaches over the clingstone varieties, if possible. Freestone peaches tend to be juicier than their clingstone cousins and are also slightly easier to work with because, as the name suggests, the pit falls easily from the peach when you cut the fruit open. No messy prying required.

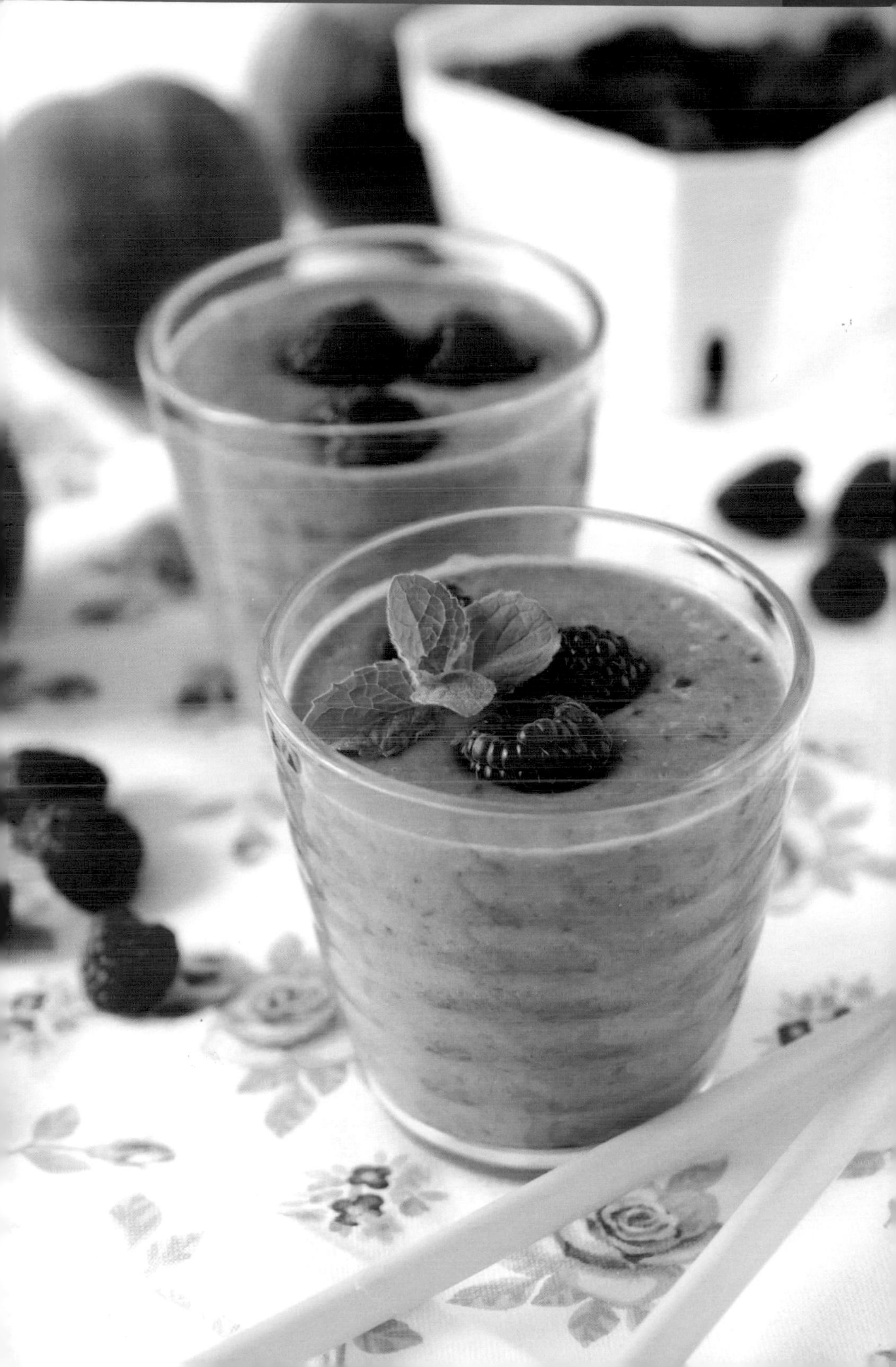

Pomegranate Berry

This fruit smoothie is a great choice for anyone who is interested in adding greens to smoothies but is hesitant to try. The rich flavours of acai, pomegranate and cherries can mask almost any green you want to add— frozen peas also work well. Or you can leave the veggies out and enjoy a tasty fruity treat. Pomegranate juice is high in cancer-fighting flavonoids, and cherries contain ellegic acid, also thought to help prevent cancer.

Frozen cherries	**2 cups**	**500 mL**
Baby spinach, optional	**1 cup**	**250 mL**
Acai powder	**1 tbsp.**	**15 mL**
Hemp protein powder	**1 tbsp.**	**15 mL**
Pomegranate berry juice	**1 cup**	**250 mL**
Ice cubes	**1 cup**	**250 mL**

Combine the cherries, spinach (if using), acai, hemp and pomegranate juice in a blender until smooth. Add the ice and blend again until smooth and icy. Makes 2 servings.

1 serving: *260 Calories; 3 g Total Fat (0 g Mono, 0 g Poly, 1 g Sat); 0 mg Cholesterol; 52 g Carbohydrate (6 g Fibre, 42 g Sugar); 7 g Protein; 35 mg Sodium*

This smoothie is also delicious if you replace the frozen cherries with fresh or frozen blueberries.

Tropical Sensation

Not only do mango, pineapple and papaya impart a taste of the tropics to your smoothie, but they also provide a wealth of health benefits. Papaya and mango contain zeaxantin, an antioxidant that protects eye health and may help prevent macular degeneration, and all three fruits are good sources of beta-carotene, which may help prevent some forms of cancer.

Chopped papaya	1 cup	250 mL
Frozen pineapple chunks	1 cup	250 mL
Frozen mango chunks	1 cup	250 mL
Chopped Brazil nuts	1/4 cup	60 mL
Lucuma powder	1 tbsp.	15 mL
Coconut milk kefir	1 cup	250 mL

Combine all the ingredients in a blender until smooth. Makes 2 servings.

1 serving: 160 Calories; 3.5 g Total Fat (0 g Mono, 0 g Poly, 3 g Sat); 0 mg Cholesterol; 32 g Carbohydrate (7 g Fibre, 20 g Sugar); 1 g Protein; 25 mg Sodium

Just one Brazil nut conatins the recommended daily value of selenium, a mineral that helps boost the immune system and regulate thyroid function.

Cherry Berry Plum

Plums are members of the *prunus* genus of plants and are closely related to peaches and nectarines. They are an excellent source of vitamin C and can help the body absorb iron. They are also high in potassium, which can help lower blood pressure and maintain heart health. The combination of strawberries, cherries and plums in this smoothie should be plenty sweet, especially if your plums are ripe and in season, but if you need a little extra sweetness, add a few more dates or a splash of maple syrup or honey.

Frozen strawberries	3/4 cup	175 mL
Frozen cherries	3/4 cup	175 mL
Dates, chopped	5	5
Fresh plums, pitted	1 1/2 cups	375 mL
Acai powder	2 tbsp.	30 mL
Chia seeds	1 tbsp.	15 mL
Water	1/2 cup	125 mL
Vanilla extract	1 tsp.	5 mL
Ice cubes	8	8

Combine the first 8 ingredients in a blender until smooth. Add the ice and blend again until smooth and icy. Makes 2 servings.

1 serving: 250 Calories; 5 g Total Fat (0 g Mono, 1.5 g Poly, 1.5 g Sat); 0 mg Cholesterol; 47 g Carbohydrate (9 g Fibre, 34 g Sugar); 4 g Protein; 20 mg Sodium

Because they are so small, a spoonful of chia seeds added to a smoothie will go almost undetected; however, the seeds have a unique ability to absorb more than eight times their weight in liquid, so any smoothie containing chia should be consumed right away as it will thicken the longer it sits.

Raspberry Orange Avocado

For anyone who is not a fan of bananas, avocado is the perfect base for a smoothie, providing a rich creamy texture. Avocado is also ranked as one of the healthiest foods you can eat; some of its benefits include helping to maintain bone health, support the digestive tract, lower cholesterol and fight some forms of cancer. If you prefer a thicker smoothie you can replace the fresh pineapple with frozen, and add a few ice cubes made of coconut water for a little tropical boost.

Frozen raspberries	2 cups	500 mL
Chopped fresh pineapple	1/2 cup	125 mL
Avocado	1/2	1/2
Chia seeds	1 tbsp.	15 mL
Freshly squeezed orange juice	1 cup	250 mL

Combine all the ingredients in a blender until smooth. Makes 2 servings.

1 serving: 240 Calories; 10 g Total Fat (5 g Mono, 2.5 g Poly, 1.5 g Sat); 0 mg Cholesterol; 40 g Carbohydrate (14 g Fibre, 21 g Sugar); 4 g Protein; 15 mg Sodium

Ice cubes are an essential part of many smoothies, so why not get a little creative with them? Make flavoured ice cubes out of pure fruit juice, coconut water or tea (or experiment with any beverage you choose) and add them to your next smoothie to give it a tasty little boost. Use an ice cube tray with a lid to keep your ice cubes fresh and prevent them from taking on other flavours in the freezer.

Cranberry Apple

The link between cranberries and urinary tract health has long been established, but researchers have recently discovered that eating cranberries can also prevent tooth decay and boost general oral health. The same micronutrients that prevent bacteria from sticking to the urinary tract walls also prevent bacteria from sticking to teeth and gums preventing cavities and perhaps even gum disease. This smoothie is on the thicker side, so feel free to thin it with a little extra almond milk or water.

Frozen cranberries	3/4 cup	175 mL
Medium red apple, cored and chopped	1	1
Frozen red grapes	1/2 cup	125 mL
Walnuts	1/4 cup	60 mL
Ground cinnamon, to taste		
Ground ginger, to taste		
Almond milk	1 cup	250 mL
Maple syrup or honey, to taste		
Ice cubes	1 cup	250 mL

1 serving: *230 Calories; 11 g Total Fat (1.5 g Mono, 7 g Poly, 1 g Sat); 0 mg Cholesterol; 33 g Carbohydrate (6 g Fibre, 23 g Sugar); 3 g Protein; 80 mg Sodium*

If you aren't already including walnuts in your diet, you should start. Not only are they high in omega-3 fatty acids, but they also contain more antioxidants than any other nut. Walnuts are high in mono- and polyunsaturated fats, which may help prevent type 2 diabetes, and they can help maintain heart health by lowering blood pressure and supporting healthy cholesterol levels. Research suggests they can also help fight inflammatory diseases such as rheumatoid arthritis.

Blueberry Chocolate Bean Smoothie

Blending beans into a smoothie might seem a little odd, but the end result is rich, creamy and loaded with nutrition. White beans such as navy or cannellini beans are excellent sources of fibre and folate, both of which are often lacking in the typical North American diet, and are high in protein, iron, potassium and manganese. They are believed to help regulate blood sugar, prevent heart disease and lower cholesterol.

Frozen blueberries	1 cup	250 mL
Cacao nibs	1/4 cup	60 mL
Canned white beans	1/4 cup	60 mL
Vanilla Greek yogurt	1/2 cup	125 mL
Almond milk	1 cup	250 mL

Combine all the ingredients in a blender until smooth. Makes 2 servings.

1 serving: 290 Calories; 11 g Total Fat (1 g Mono, 0 g Poly, 6 g Sat); 5 mg Cholesterol; 28 g Carbohydrate (9 g Fibre, 15 g Sugar); 14 g Protein; 170 mg Sodium

This is another smoothie that lends itself to hiding greens; baby spinach works especially well.

Raspberry Pear

Pears and raspberries work together in this smoothie to create a sweet-tart sensation that really satisfies. Like raspberries, pears are high in vitamin C, but they also contain boron, a trace mineral that helps the body absorb calcium and magnesium and may help prevent osteoporosis, arthritis and hypothyroidism. Boron also helps alleviate the affects of rheumatoid arthritis.

Fresh ripe pear, chopped	1	1
Frozen raspberries	1 cup	250 mL
Hemp seeds	1 tbsp.	15 mL
Vanilla Greek yogurt	1/2 cup	125 mL
Almond milk	1/2 cup	125 mL
Ice cubes	8	8

Combine the first 5 ingredients in a blender until smooth. Add the ice and blend again until smooth and icy. Makes 2 servings.

1 serving: 190 Calories; 3 g Total Fat (0 g Mono, 0 g Poly, 0.5 g Sat); trace Cholesterol; 33 g Carbohydrate (9 g Fibre, 18 g Sugar); 10 g Protein; 55 mg Sodium

Although hemp and marijuana both come from the same plant, hemp does not contain the same levels of tetrahydrocannabinol (THC), the psychoactive chemical that causes the marijuana "high."

Apricot Cherry Delight

This smoothie could have been named "antioxidant delight" with the combination of antioxidant-rich apricots, cherries, chia seeds and almond butter. Or perhaps "calcium delight," as almonds, chia and apricots are great sources of this mineral as well. Apricots are also especially high in beta-carotene, which is known to help prevent heart disease.

Fresh ripe apricots, pitted	6	6
Frozen cherries	1 1/2 cups	375 mL
Almond butter	1 tbsp.	15 mL
Chia seeds	1 tbsp.	15 mL
Vanilla extract	1/4 tsp.	1 mL
Coconut milk (boxed variety)	1 cup	250 mL
Maple syrup or honey, to taste		
Ice cubes	8	8

Combine the first 7 ingredients in a blender until smooth. Add the ice and blend again until smooth and icy. Makes 2 servings.

1 serving: 120 Calories; 4 g Total Fat (0 g Mono, 1.5 g Poly, 2 g Sat); 0 mg Cholesterol; 20 g Carbohydrate (5 g Fibre, 14 g Sugar); 2 g Protein; 15 mg Sodium

Unlike flax seeds, chia seeds do not need to be ground before the body can obtain their full nutritional benefits. Ground chia is commercially available, though, and can be used interchangeably with chia seeds in smoothies.

Blackberry Peach

Kefir is a fermented milk product that is rich with probiotics, containing almost three times as much as can be found in yogurt. Kefir is perhaps best known for aiding digestion, but it is also high in protein, which is necessary for healthy bones and tissue, and phosphorus, an important mineral for cell growth. Kefir has a distinct flavour that can range from tart to sour; depending on how tart your blackberries are, you may need to sweeten things up with a little maple syrup or honey. Use coconut kefir if you want to avoid dairy.

Chopped fresh ripe peaches	2 cups	500 mL
Frozen blackberries	1 cup	250 mL
Chopped pecans	1/4 cup	60 mL
Kefir	1 cup	250 mL
Maple syrup or honey, to taste		
Ice cubes	8	8

Combine the first 5 ingredients in a blender until smooth. Add the ice and blend again until smooth and icy. Makes 2 servings.

1 serving: 250 Calories; 12 g Total Fat (6 g Mono, 3.5 g Poly, 1.5 g Sat); trace Cholesterol; 33 g Carbohydrate (8 g Fibre, 26 g Sugar); 9 g Protein; 65 mg Sodium

Frozen fruit is often seen as the ugly sister of fresh fruit, but it can actually be the better choice, nutritionally speaking. Fruit begins to lose nutrients from the moment it is picked. Frozen fruit is picked at the peak of ripeness (when it has the most nutrients) and is flash-frozen soon after being harvested, basically locking in its nutrients. However, unless you are buying from local farmer's markets, much of the fresh fruit available has been picked before it is ripe and transported vast distances to reach grocery store shelves, ripening (and losing nutrients) along the way.

Strawberry Mango Guava

Unless you live in the tropics, guava might not be a fruit you typically see on the supermarket shelves, but it is worth seeking out. Guava fruit is high in fibre, vitamins A and C, manganese and lycopene and is a good source of folate and potassium. It is believed to help boost immunity, improve circulation, regulate blood pressure and combat certain forms of cancer. Guava juice does not contain the fibre found in the fruit, but it still provides many of the same health benefits. In this smoothie, it combines with the coconut water, mango and strawberry to create a healthy version of a fruit slushie, perfect for a hot summer day.

Frozen strawberries	1 1/2 cups	375 mL
Frozen mango chunks	1 cup	250 mL
Chia seeds	1 tbsp.	15 mL
Guava juice	3/4 cup	175 mL
Coconut water	1/2 cup	125 mL
Ice cubes	8	8

Combine the first 5 ingredients in a blender until smooth. Add the ice and blend again until smooth and icy. Makes 2 servings.

1 serving: 360 Calories; 4 g Total Fat (0 g Mono, 3 g Poly, 0 g Sat); 0 mg Cholesterol; 81 g Carbohydrate (14 g Fibre, 63 g Sugar); 5 g Protein; 140 mg Sodium

Coconut water has gained a lot of attention lately as a super-hydrator, said to be comparable to sports drinks for replacing electrolytes lost during intense exercise. These claims have yet to be substantiated by the scientific community, but coconut water is still an  excellent ingredient to use in smoothies. It provides a subtle sweetness without adding refined sugars, and gives the smoothie deliciously tropical undertones.

Melon Berry

Cantaloupe is the perfect summer treat. With its high water content it helps keep the body hydrated, and it provides a good dose of beta-carotene, fibre, potassium and vitamin C. Try freezing your ripe cantaloupe to give this smoothie a thicker, milkshake-like consistency. Strawberries would also be delicious in place of the raspberries.

Chopped cantaloupe	1 cup	250 mL
Frozen raspberries	1 1/2 cups	375 mL
Goji berries	3 tbsp.	45 mL
Green tea, chilled	1/2 cup	125 mL

Combine all the ingredients in a blender until smooth. Makes 2 servings.

1 serving: 110 Calories; 1 g Total Fat (0 g Mono, 0 g Poly, 0 g Sat); 0 mg Cholesterol; 25 g Carbohydrate (7 g Fibre, 16 g Sugar); 3 g Protein; 35 mg Sodium

A cantaloupe's flavour comes from being allowed to properly ripen on the vine, so make sure you choose a ripe one. It should have a slightly musky odour; odourless melons will lack in flavour. Another way to check for ripeness is to push gently on the melon's base, opposite the stem. It should give a little without being too soft. Soft, lumpy melons are past their prime and will be quite watery.

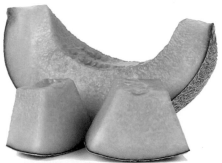

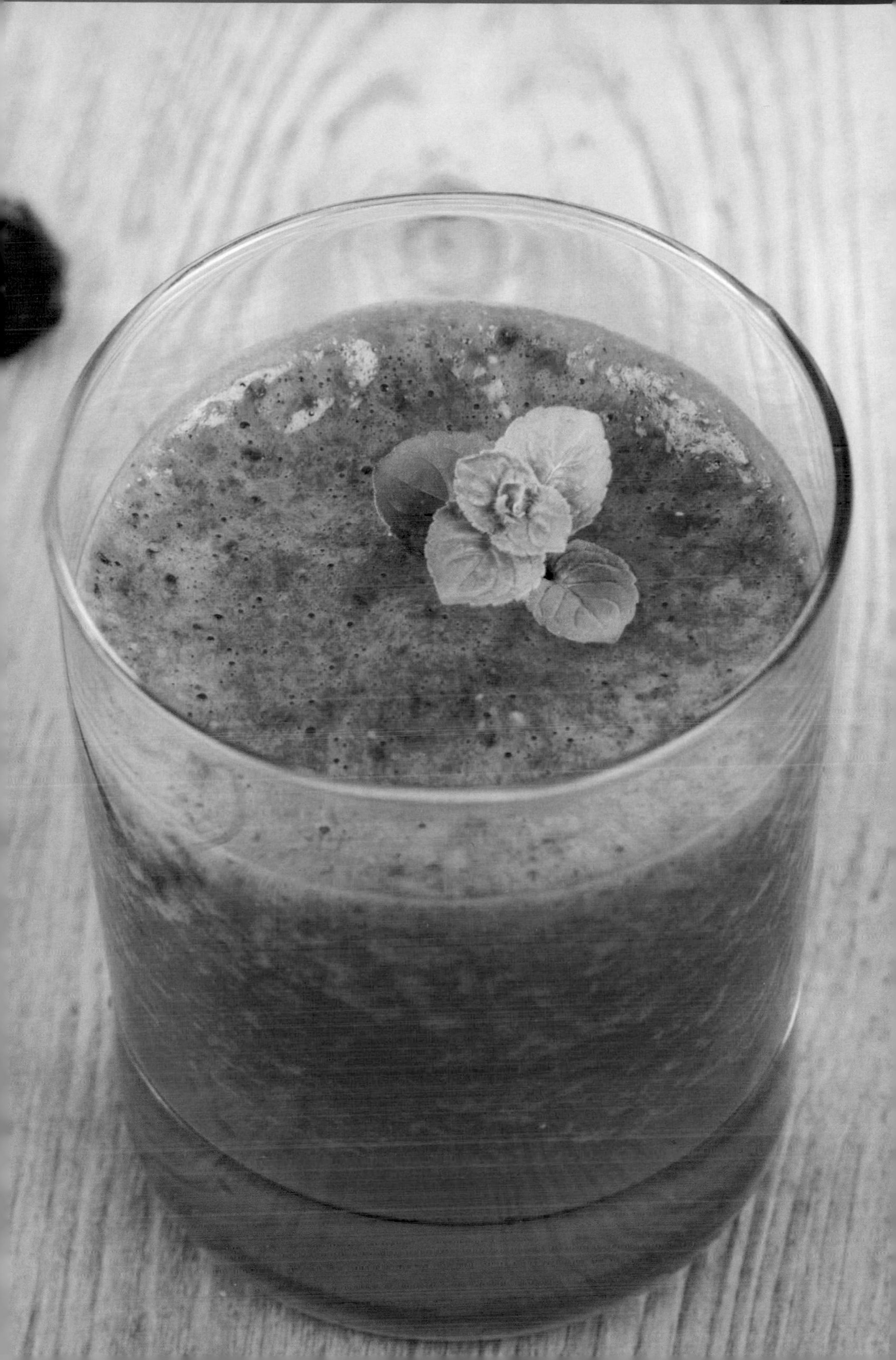

Lychee Coconut

Native to China, fresh lychees can be difficult to find in North America, but canned lychees are readily available and can be used in this smoothie if you can't find fresh ones. Lychees are high in vitamin C, containing more than 100 percent of the recommended daily value in just one serving. They also have anti-inflammatory properties and are a good source of rutin, a bioflavonoid that helps strengthen blood vessels.

Fresh lychees, pitted	9	9
Chopped ripe pear	1 cup	250 mL
Hemp seeds	1/4 cup	60 mL
Coconut milk (boxed variety)	1/2 cup	125 mL
Green tea, cooled	1/2 cup	125 mL
Ice cubes	8	8

Combine the first 5 ingredients in a blender until smooth. Add the ice and blend again until smooth and icy. Makes 2 servings.

1 serving: 170 Calories; 8 g Total Fat (3 g Mono, 0 g Poly, 1.5 g Sat); 0 mg Cholesterol; 21 g Carbohydrate (4 g Fibre, 15 g Sugar); 6 g Protein; 5 mg Sodium

For the best flavour, choose a very ripe pear for this smoothie. Ripe pears are at their peak sweetness and help offset the slight bitterness of the green tea.

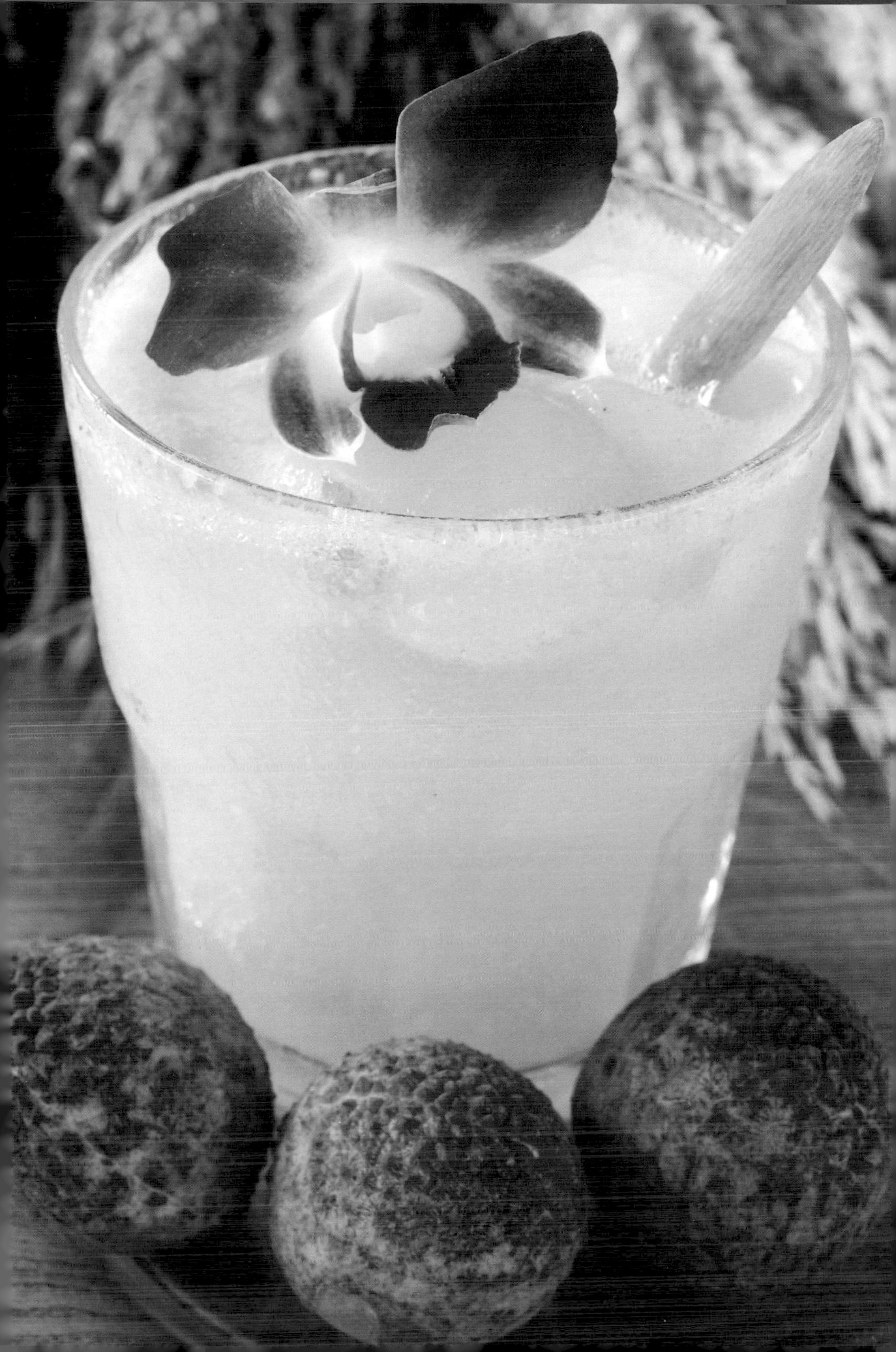

Raspberry Grapefruit

Grapefruit is one of those fruits you either love or hate; it is not the first fruit you think of to add to a smoothie. With its distinct flavour, grapefruit can overpower all other ingredients alongside it, but in this blend, the sweetness of the apple, banana and mango helps smooth everything out. Grapefruit may help prevent the hardening of arteries, and pink grapefruit contains lycopene, an antioxidant with cancer-fighting properites.

Small pink grapefruit, peeled and seeded	1	1
Frozen banana	1	1
Medium red apple, seeded and chopped	1/2	1/2
Frozen raspberries	1 cup	250 mL
Wheatgrass powder	1 tsp.	5 mL
Ground flaxseed	1 tbsp.	15 mL
Vanilla Greek yogurt	1/2 cup	125 mL
Honey	1 tsp.	5 mL

Combine all the ingredients in a blender until smooth. Makes 2 servings.

1 serving: *270 Calories; 8 g Total Fat (0 g Mono, 1.5 g Poly, 4 g Sat); 15 mg Cholesterol; 46 g Carbohydrate (10 g Fibre, 29 g Sugar); 6 g Protein; 35 mg Sodium*

Flaxseed is perhaps best known as an excellent source of omega-3 fatty acids, but it is also loaded with antioxidants, most notably lignans, which have powerful cancer-fighting properties. It is also high in fibre, which as well as keeping you regular can help ward off diseases of the colon, lower cholesterol and stabilize blood sugar.

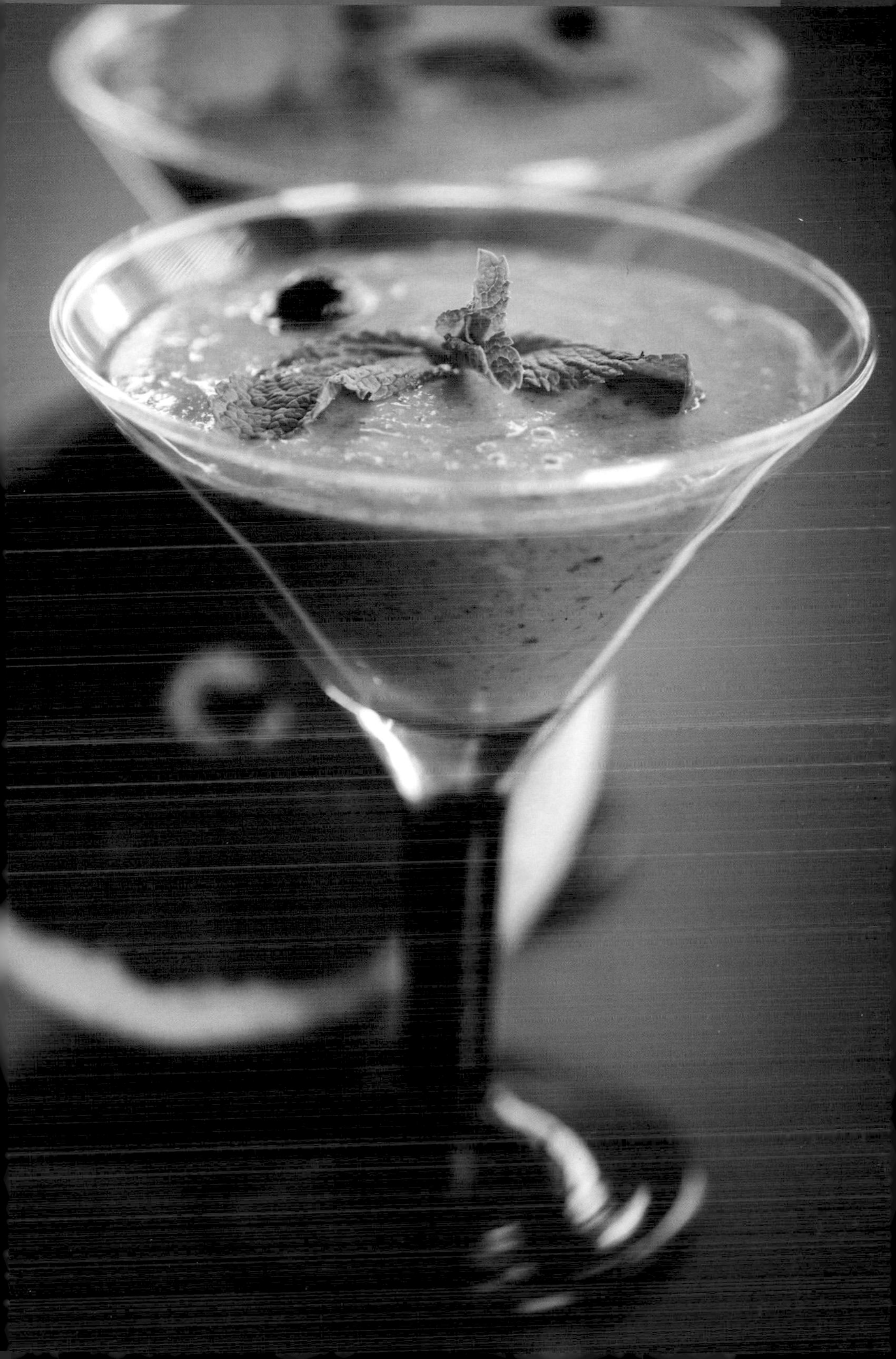

Strawberry Kiwi

Strawberry and kiwi are two fruits that are just meant to be eaten together, and the classic sweet-tart combination works especially well in a smoothie. Both kiwi and strawberries are excellent sources of vitamin C and are high in antioxidants, helping to protect the body from damage caused by free radicals. The chia seeds, though practically undetectable, provide a healthy dose of protein and omega-3 fatty acids.

Frozen banana	1	1
Kiwi fruit, peeled	2	2
Frozen strawberries	1 cup	250 mL
Maple syrup or honey, to taste		
Chia seeds	1 tbsp.	15 mL
Coconut water	1 cup	250 mL

Combine all the ingredients in a blender until smooth. Makes 2 servings.

1 serving: 200 Calories; 2.5 g Total Fat (0 g Mono, 1.5 g Poly, 0 g Sat); 0 mg Cholesterol; 45 g Carbohydrate (9 g Fibre, 27 g Sugar); 4 g Protein; 130 mg Sodium

Using frozen bananas instead of fresh makes for a rich, creamy, milkshake-like smoothie. For maximum sweetness, choose bananas that are overripe. Remove the browning peel, slice the bananas into chunks and place them on a baking tray in the freezer. Once they are frozen, you can put the chunks into a resealable freezer bag, where they will last for 2 to 3 months.

Black 'n' Blue

Is there anything better than a berry smoothie? This delicious drink gets its beautiful, rich colour from the blackberries, blueberries and acai powder. Acai's delicate berry flavour adds depth to this smoothie, while the avocado makes it creamy without overpowering the other flavours, as banana would. Berries are some of the most nutritious fruits you can eat, and blueberries in particular have numerous health benefits. They are thought to help lower cholesterol, help build and maintain strong bones, protect against diabetes, and recent studies suggest they may even offer a protective factor against Parkinson's disease and Alzheimer's.

Frozen blackberries	1 cup	250 mL
Frozen blueberries	1 cup	250 mL
Avocado	1/2	1/2
Wheatgrass powder	1 tsp.	5 mL
Acai powder	1 tbsp.	15 mL
Coconut water	1 cup	250 mL

Combine all the ingredients in a blender until smooth. Makes 2 servings.

1 serving: 210 Calories; 9 g Total Fat (4.5 g Mono, 1 g Poly, 2 g Sat); 0 mg Cholesterol; 29 g Carbohydrate (12 g Fibre, 14 g Sugar); 4 g Protein; 140 mg Sodium

Green vegetables get their colour from chlorophyll, a pigment that traps the sun's energy and, through photosynthesis, turns it into fuel for the plant. Chlorophyll-rich foods are highly nutritious and should make up a large part of a healthy diet. However, one can eat only so much salad. If you've had your fill of leafy greens (or have none on hand), reach for the wheatgrass powder instead. Ounce per ounce, wheatgrass is comparable in nutritional content to spinach and broccoli, but it is practically undetectable in a smoothie.

Grape Berry Plum

Although they often make the "dirty list" of the most pesticide-sprayed fruits, grapes are also considered some of the most nutritiously dense fruits you can eat. Grapes are loaded with polyphenols, antioxidants that may reduce the risk of cancer and cardiovascular disease. Red varieties are touted as the more nutritious option because they contain more antioxidants than the green varieties. Resveratrol, a polyphenol found in the skin of red grapes has received a great deal of attention for its possible roll in maintaining heart health. Red grapes are also an excellent source of potassium, which protects heart health and helps regulate blood pressure. We've used frozen grapes to give this smoothie a thicker, frostier texture, but regular grapes would work well, too.

Frozen seedless red grapes	1 cup	250 mL
Frozen raspberries	3/4 cup	75 mL
Chopped plums	1 1/2 cups	375 mL
Maqui berry powder	2 tsp.	10 mL
Prepared green tea, chilled	1 cup	250 mL

Combine all the ingredients in a blender until smooth. Makes 2 servings.

1 serving: *140 Calories; 1 g Total Fat (0 g Mono, 0 g Poly, 0 g Sat); 0 mg Cholesterol; 36 g Carbohydrate (6 g Fibre, 28 g Sugar); 2 g Protein; 0 mg Sodium*

Maqui berries are small purple berries native to South America that are renowned for having the highest levels of antioxidants found in any fruit. The actual berry is not readily available outside of South America, but a freeze-dried maqui powder can be found in many organic supermarkets or online. It has a mild flavour that, in smoothies, blends nicely with other types of fruit.

Mango Peach Goji

This smoothie tastes best made in summer with fresh peaches that are at their peak of ripeness. Although you could make the smoothie with frozen peaches, nothing compares to the flavour and juiciness of a fresh ripe peach. You could also substitute nectarines, which are really just fuzzless peaches. When removing the pit, cut your peach open over the blender's pitcher so that you won't lose any of the juice. The combination of peaches and mango should give this smoothie enough sweetness, but if you need a little more, add a splash of maple syrup or a bit of honey.

Fresh ripe peaches, chopped	3	3
Frozen mango	1 cup	250 mL
Goji berries	3 tbsp.	45 mL
Coconut milk (boxed variety)	1 1/2 cups	375 mL
Vanilla extract	1/2 tsp.	2 mL
Maple syrup or honey, to taste		
Ice cubes	8	8

Combine the first 6 ingredients in a blender until smooth. Add the ice and blend again until smooth and icy. Makes 2 servings.

1 serving: 210 Calories; 7 g Total Fat (0 g Mono, 0 g Poly, 6 g Sat); 0 mg Cholesterol; 35 g Carbohydrate (4 g Fibre, 30 g Sugar); 3 g Protein; 60 mg Sodium

Mango is an excellent choice of fruit to use as a base for a smoothie in place of banana. Frozen mango in particular gives a smoothie a rich creaminess, but its mild flavour will not overpower the other ingredients.

Strawberry Apricot

Although they are now available year-round in grocery stores, the tastiest, most nutritious apricots usually appear on store shelves between May and August. The best way to choose a ripe apricot is to give it the sniff test—it should have a sweet, slightly floral scent. Apricots are an excellent source of beta carotene, which is believed to help prevent heart disease, and they are a good source of calcium. In this smoothie, the apricot's sweet-tart flavour helps tame the sweetness of the strawberries and mango. If the end result is not sweet enough for your taste, throw in a few dates or dried apricots, or a splash of maple syrup.

Fresh ripe apricots, pitted and chopped	3	3
Frozen mango	1/2 cup	125 mL
Frozen strawberries	2 cups	500 mL
Ground flaxseed	1 tbsp.	15 mL
Maqui berry powder	2 tsp.	10 mL
Coconut or coconut-almond milk	3/4 cup	175 mL

Combine all the ingredients in a blender until smooth. Makes 2 servings.

1 serving: 150 Calories; 4 g Total Fat (0.5 g Mono, 1.5 g Poly, 1.5 g Sat); 0 mg Cholesterol; 28 g Carbohydrate (7 g Fibre, 20 g Sugar); 3 g Protein; 10 mg Sodium

Unlike many other types of fruit, strawberries do not continue to ripen after they have been picked, so choose bright red strawberries and give any with a greenish tinge a pass.

Blueberry Watermelon

   Watermelon is made up of more than 90 percent water, so it is no wonder that it is such a refreshing snack on a hot summer's day. Because of its high water content and electrolyte balance, watermelon can help prevent dehydration and flush toxins from the kidneys. It is also an excellent source of lycopene, a powerful antioxidant that may protect against strokes.

Frozen blueberries	1 1/2 cups	375 mL
Chopped seedless watermelon	1 cup	250 mL
Frozen green grapes	1/2 cup	125 mL
Acai powder	1 tbsp.	15 mL
Ice cubes	1 cup	250 mL

Combine the first 4 ingredients in a blender until smooth. Add the ice and blend again until smooth and icy. Makes 2 servings.

1 serving: 140 Calories; 2 g Total Fat (0 g Mono, 0 g Poly, 1 g Sat); 0 mg Cholesterol; 30 g Carbohydrate (4 g Fibre, 22 g Sugar); 2 g Protein; 10 mg Sodium

Though most people usually eat only the flesh of the watermelon, the rind is edible as well. It is a good source of chlorophyll and is high in citrulline, an amino acid that is thought to reduce muscle pain.

Superfood Add-ins

Although fruit and veggie smoothies are already an excellent source of nutrition, there are a few simple ingredients you can add to pack in even more nutrients. Here are some of our favourites.

Acai berry powder: acai berries are small, dark purplish-blue berries from the acai palm tree, native to South America. Research suggests that acai berries contain more antioxidants than any other berry. They also contain omega-3 fatty acids and oleic acid, and are an excellent source of iron, calcium and fibre. Acai berries have a soft berry flavour that combines well with other berries, cherries and pomegranate. They are not overly sweet and in fact contain less sugar than most other fruits. You are not likely to find the actual acai berries outside of South America, so look for the freeze-dried powder (the form used in this book), juice or frozen pulp.

Cacao/cacao nibs: dark chocolate has enjoyed a change in status recently; where it was once considered a junk food that is best avoided, it is now thought to be a boon to one's health, imparting surprising health benefits. The health benefits of chocolate come from the humble cacao bean, from which chocolate is made. Cacao beans are high in antioxidants, particularly a type of flavonoid called flavanols that are thought to help prevent cancer and heart disease, reduce the risk of Alzheimer's, lower blood pressure and improve circulation. The cacao bean is also high in fibre and magnesium and is a source of calcium, iron and protein. Cacao nibs are cacao beans that have been roasted, then peeled and chopped into smaller bits. Cacao powder is essentially ground cacao nibs and is much like cocoa powder except that it is less processed, so it retains more of the nutrients of the cacao bean, and it is slightly more bitter.

Chia seeds: the chia plant is native to Central America, where it has been a staple for centuries. Historically it was grown by the Aztecs, who harvested the seeds and ate them as a cereal. Chia seeds have been garnering much attention lately as a superstar of nutrition. They are an excellent source of omega-3 fatty acids, protein, iron, calcium and antioxidants.

Flaxseed: flaxseed has been part of the human diet since the Stone Age, and with good reason. An excellent source of antioxidants, fibre, omega-3 fatty acids and manganese, flaxseed supports good health in many ways. It has anti-inflammatory properties, can help stabilize blood sugar, can help lower levels of LDL (or so-called "bad") cholesterol and is thought to prevent many types of cancer by preventing cancerous cells from growing. Flaxseed is also high in lignans, compounds that help balance hormone levels and may help reduce hot flashes in postmenopausal women.

Goji berries: native to the Himalayas, goji berries have a long history of culinary and medicinal use in China. The fresh berries do not travel well, but a dried version is readily available online or in natural food stores throughout North America. Goji berries have been credited with a vast array of health benefits, many of which are unsubstantiated, but it is a highly nutritious berry. As members of the nightshade family, goji berries are high in carotenoids, particularly lutein and lycopene, both of which help maintain eye health. The berries are also high in fibre and are an excellent source of antioxidants, including vitamin C. Be sure to buy organic goji berries because there has been some controversy about the overuse of pesticides and fungicides in goji cultivation.

Hemp seeds: these small, nutty tasting seeds are garnering a lot of attention among the health conscious of late, and with good reason. They are an excellent source of complete protein, meaning that they contain all 9 essential amino acids, and are particularly high in omega-3 fatty acids. They are also a good source of iron, magnesium and zinc.

Lucuma powder: native to the Andes of Peru, Chile and Ecuador, the lucuma fruit looks much like a smooth skinned avocado on the outside, but the flesh is a soft shade of orange, somewhat like a cantaloupe. Its flavour is difficult to describe but has been said to taste like a cross between mango and sweet potato with notes of caramel or maple. You are unlikely to find lucuma fruit outside of South America, but as with acai berries, the freeze-dried powder is available in natural food stores and online. Lucuma is a good source of beta-carotene and B vitamins and also contains calcium and iron. Despite its sweet flavour, lucuma is a low-sugar fruit and is low on the glycemic index. As such, it is perfect for adding to smoothies, where it imparts natural sweetness without adding refined sugar.

Spirulina: a type of blue-green algae, spirulina is an excellent source of concentrated nutrients. With less than a teaspoon of powder, spirulina provides an excellent source of protein and chlorophyll, and it is also high in iron and vitamins A, B, D and K. Be choosy about where you get your spirulina, though, because algae is a microfilter and as such can take on the toxins from the water where it grows. Look look for spirulina that has been tested for purity.

Wheatgrass powder: as the name suggests, wheatgrass powder is freeze-dried grass from the wheat family that is crushed into a powdered form, perfect for adding to smoothies. This nutrient-rich powder is high in chlorophyll, which may help reduce the risk of cancer, particularly colon cancer, and is an excellent source of vitamins A, C and E. It also contains calcium, iron and magnesium. Research suggests that wheatgrass may promote good digestion and help alleviate constipation and reflux.

Strawberry Cucumber

Made up of about 96 percent water, cucumber is an excellent hydrator, and it is also a diuretic, which can help flush excess salt and toxins from the body. Cucumber's main claim to nutritional fame, though, may be its high levels of cucurbitacins—phytonutrients in the cucurbitaceae family of plants that protect the plants from being eaten by browsing herbivores. Research shows that cucurbitacins might also protect us from cancer by inhibiting the growth of cancer cells. Mint and cucumber are a natural pairing and really complement the strawberry in this smoothie.

Frozen strawberries	2 cups	500 mL
Peeled, chopped cucumber	2 cups	500 mL
Chopped celery	1/4 cup	60 mL
Finely chopped fresh mint	1/2 tsp.	2 mL
Almond butter	1 tbsp.	15 mL
Lime juice	2 tbsp.	30 mL
Water	1 cup	250 mL

Combine all the ingredients in a blender until smooth. Makes 2 servings.

1 serving: 150 Calories; 4.5 g Total Fat (0 g Mono, 0 g Poly, 0 g Sat); 0 mg Cholesterol; 27 g Carbohydrate (4 g Fibre, 17 g Sugar); 4 g Protein; 15 mg Sodium

Cucumber, like mint, is a natural breath freshener. Holding a slice against the roof of your mouth with your tongue for a minute or so will kill the bacteria that cause bad breath.

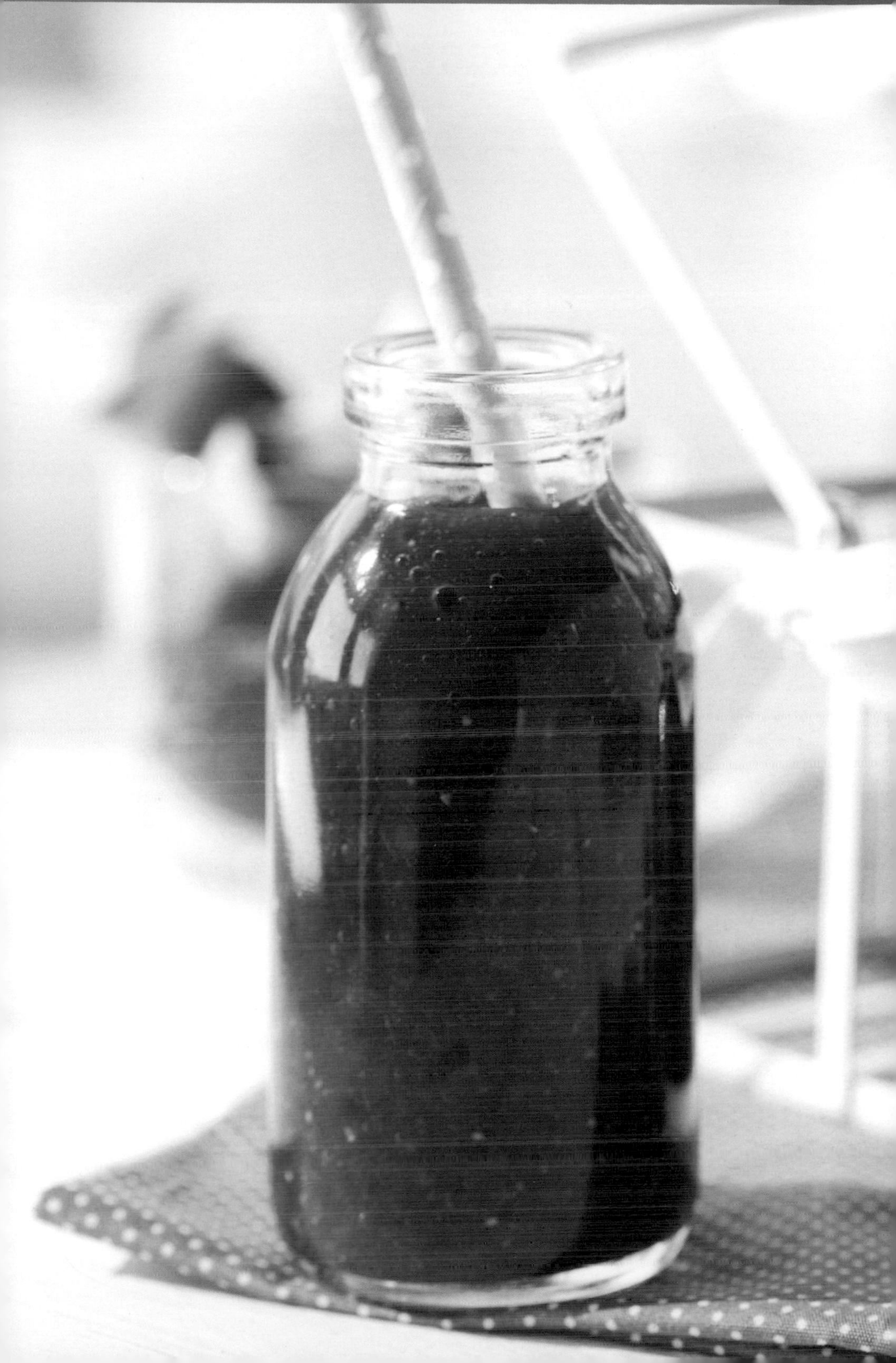

Ginger Pear Green Smoothie

Ginger has been grown for centuries and was one of the most important trade goods imported into the Roman empire, though the Romans used it for its medicinal benefits, not to season their cooking. Ginger is well known as a digestive aid and for helping to relieve nausea. It also has anti-inflammatory properties, which may help relieve the pain of rheumatoid arthritis and osteoarthritis.

Dates, chopped	2	2
Frozen spinach	2 cups	500 mL
Fresh ripe pear, chopped	1	1
Grated ginger root	1/2 tsp.	2 mL
Chia seeds	1 tbsp.	15 mL
Coconut water	1 1/2 cups	375 mL
Lemon juice	1 tbsp.	15 mL

Combine all the ingredients in a blender until smooth. Makes 2 servings.

1 serving: 300 Calories; 3 g Total Fat (0 g Mono, 2.5 g Poly, 0 g Sat); 0 mg Cholesterol; 61 g Carbohydrate (20 g Fibre, 36 g Sugar); 11 g Protein; 450 mg Sodium

The Medjool date is considered the king of dates because of its soft flesh and exceptional sweetness—making it a perfect natural sweetener for a smoothie. The flesh gets finely chopped in the blender, giving the smoothie little nuggets of sweetness. If you don't have Medjool dates, any other variety will work as well.

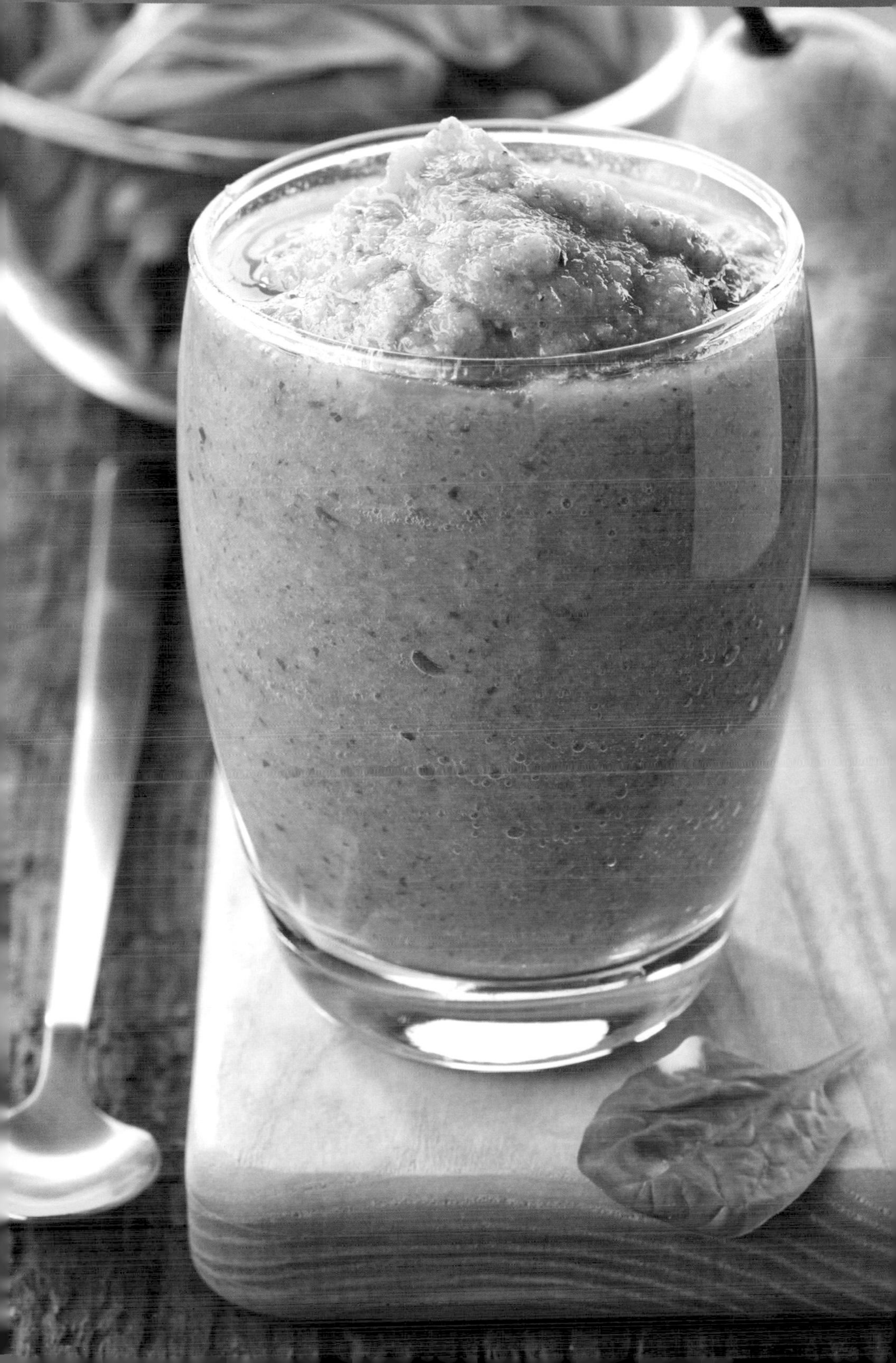

Blueberry Avocado

Blueberries are one of the most popular berries in North America, second only to the strawberry. Although they were used extensively by First Nations peoples throughout history, blueberries have been cultivated only since the 1920s. The berries get their colour from anthocyanins, a type of flavonoid known for antioxidant and anti-inflammatory properties. In this smoothie, the frozen berries and avocado create a rich, creamy smoothie and make the spinach practically undetectable.

Frozen blueberries	1 cup	250 mL
Baby spinach	1 cup	250 mL
Avocado	1/2	1/2
Hemp seeds	1 tbsp.	15 mL
Ground cinnamon	1/4 tsp.	1 mL
Dates, chopped	3	3
Vanilla extract	1 tsp.	5 mL
Almond milk	1 cup	250 mL
Ice cubes	6	6

Combine the first 8 ingredients in a blender until smooth. Add the ice and blend again until smooth and icy. Makes 2 servings.

1 serving: 220 Calories; 10 g Total Fat (4.5 g Mono, 1 g Poly, 1 g Sat); 0 mg Cholesterol; 28 g Carbohydrate (8 g Fibre, 16 g Sugar); 7 g Protein; 90 mg Sodium

Avocados turn from dark green to almost black and go soft when they are ripe. Look for rinds that are dark and flesh that yields just slightly to gentle pressure. Very soft avocados are probably overripe and may be brown inside.

Chocolate Beet

Roasting beets brings out their natural sweetness and makes all the difference in this smoothie. Raw beets can give smoothies an earthiness that, while not unpleasant, can be an acquired taste. Here the roasted beets combine with the cacao powder, dates and almond-coconut milk to make a rich, creamy smoothie that is worthy of dessert. Beets are high in fibre, vitamin A and potassium, which helps to lower blood pressure and regulate metabolism.

Dates, chopped	4	4
Roasted beets	1/2 cup	125 mL
Cacao powder	3 tbsp.	45 mL
Almond-coconut milk	1 cup	250 mL
Vanilla extract	1/2 tsp.	2 mL
Maple syrup or honey, to taste		
Ice cubes	12	12

Combine the first 6 ingredients in a blender until smooth. Add the ice and blend again until smooth and icy. Makes 2 servings.

1 serving: 280 Calories; 6 g Total Fat (1.5 g Mono, 2.5 g Poly, 1.5 g Sat); 0 mg Cholesterol; 54 g Carbohydrate (13 g Fibre, 34 g Sugar); 14 g Protein; 115 mg Sodium

Cacao beans were so prized by the Aztecs that they became a form of currency, and all taxes had to be paid in cacao beans.

Sweet Potato Pineapple

I know what you're thinking. Sweet potato? Really? Yup, sweet potato. Really. Mashed sweet potato is the perfect base for a fruity smoothie, creating a sinfully creamy shake while adding a wealth of antioxidants, particularly beta-carotene. The combination the sweet potato, mango and pineapple give this smoothie a real tropical feel. Thin the smoothie with a little of the reserved pineapple juice if it's too thick.

Canned pineapple chunks, drained (juice reserved)	1 cup	250 mL
Frozen mango	3/4 cup	175 mL
Mashed sweet potato	1 cup	250 mL
Ground cinnamon	1/2 tsp.	2 mL
Vanilla Greek yogurt	1/2 cup	125 mL

Combine all the ingredients in a blender until smooth. Makes 2 servings.

1 serving: 430 Calories; 4 g Total Fat (0 g Mono, 0 g Poly, 2 g Sat); 15 mg Cholesterol; 96 g Carbohydrate (9 g Fibre, 67 g Sugar); 9 g Protein; 150 mg Sodium

Greek yogurt has about twice as much protein and half the lactose found in regular yogurt. It is made by straining the liquid whey and lactose from regular yogurt, essentially concentrating the nutrition into a thick, creamy "super yogurt." It is an excellent way to add more protein to your diet, but watch out for brands that have added sweeteners.

Strawberry Banana Cauliflower

As a member of the brassica family, cauliflower is a powerhouse of nutrition and is loaded with cancer-fighting properties. Nutrition aside, however, one of cauliflower's best qualities is its malleability. Cooked cauliflower can be mashed like potatoes, grated and pan fried like rice, or in this case, blended into a smoothie, and no one will be the wiser. The mild flavour of the cauliflower takes backstage to the bolder flavours of the banana and strawberries, and the blended florets give the smoothie a rich, creamy texture.

Frozen strawberries	**2 cups**	**500 mL**
Frozen banana	**1**	**1**
Steamed cauliflower, cooled	**1 cup**	**250 mL**
Chia seeds	**1 tbsp.**	**15 mL**
Water	**1 cup**	**250 mL**
Maple syrup	**1 tsp.**	**5 mL**
Ice cubes	**8**	**8**

Combine the first 6 ingredients in a blender until smooth. Add the ice and blend again until smooth and icy. Makes 2 servings.

1 serving: 140 Calories; 2 g Total Fat (0 g Mono, 1.5 g Poly, 0 g Sat); 0 mg Cholesterol; 31 g Carbohydrate (7 g Fibre, 17 g Sugar); 3 g Protein; 20 mg Sodium

Although white cauliflower is the most common, there are also green, orange, purple, yellow and brown varieties.

Pineapple Papaya with Bok Choy

Bok choy is a member of the brassica family, renowned for its high levels of antioxidants and folate and for its cancer-fighting properties. Vegetables in the brassica family are high in glucosinolates, sulphur-rich compounds that help prevent numerous forms of cancer including breast, bladder, liver and stomach cancer. Bok choy has a mild flavour in smoothies, slightly stronger than spinach but much less bitter than kale. In this smoothie, its slight bitterness is masked by the sweetness of the pineapple and papaya.

Frozen pineapple chunks	1 cup	250 mL
Frozen banana	1	1
Celery stalks, chopped	2	2
Chopped baby bok choy	2 cups	500 mL
Papaya, cubed	1 cup	250 mL
Chia seeds	1 tbsp.	15 mL
Coconut milk (boxed variety)	1 cup	250 mL

Combine all the ingredients in a blender until smooth. Makes 2 servings.

1 serving: *180 Calories; 4 g Total Fat (0 g Mono, 1.5 g Poly, 2 g Sat); 0 mg Cholesterol; 36 g Carbohydrate (7 g Fibre, 20 g Sugar); 4 g Protein; 105 mg Sodium*

Adding celery to a smoothie boosts the fibre content and helps cut the sweetness of the other fruits, but tread lightly if you are a green smoothie newbie. Celery has a distinct flavour that can easily overpower the other ingredients. One or two stalks is usually enough, and it is best to combine celery with sweet fruits such as pineapple, red grapes or strawberries.

Berry Dandelion

Dandelion greens are another great green to add to smoothies. Loaded with chlorophyll, vitamins A, B6, C and K, iron, calcium, potassium, manganese and folate, to name but a few, dandelion greens are a powerhouse of nutrition. When you think about all the nutrients they contain, it's a shame that we have such a negative attitude about these humble little plants when we see them growing on our lawn.

If you are new to dandelion greens, you might want to use half spinach, half dandelion greens in this smoothie until you are accustomed to their flavour. For the berries, a mix of strawberries, blueberries, blackberries and raspberries would taste great. Add a little maple syrup if the berries you use are not sweet enough.

Frozen mixed berries	1 cup	250 mL
Frozen very ripe banana	1	1
Dandelion greens	1 cup	250 mL
Vanilla Greek yogurt	1/2 cup	125 mL
Unsweetened almond milk	1 cup	250 mL
Ice cubes	8	8

Combine the first 5 ingredients in a blender until smooth. Add the ice and blend again until smooth and icy. Makes 2 servings.

1 serving: 200 Calories; 4.5 g Total Fat (0.5 g Mono, 1.5 g Poly, 1.5 g Sat); 5 mg Cholesterol; 33 g Carbohydrate (6 g Fibre, 20 g Sugar); 9 g Protein; 75 mg Sodium

Dandelion greens can be quite bitter, so you want to be sure your banana is very ripe; the sweetness will help to balance the greens. Alternatively, you could blanch the greens before adding them to the smoothie, which helps cut their bitterness.

Waldorf Salad Smoothie

All the flavours of the classic salad in a green smoothie. Waldorf salad dates back to the 1890s, when the maitre d' tossed together some chopped apple, celery and mayonnaise and served it on a bed of lettuce. The walnuts and grapes were a later addition. We've replaced the more traditional lemon juice with orange to smooth out the flavour of the romaine and add a bit of sweetness. Avocado gives the smoothie its creaminess, in place of the salad's traditional mayo.

Walnuts	1/4 cup	60 mL
Pineapple	1 cup	250 mL
Medium apple, cored and chopped	1	1
Celery stalks, chopped	4	4
Avocado	1/2	1/2
Red grapes	2 cups	500 mL
Romaine lettuce	1/2 cup	125 mL
Freshly squeezed orange juice	2/3 cup	150 mL

Combine all the ingredients in a blender until smooth. Makes 2 servings.

1 serving: 410 Calories; 18 g Total Fat (6 g Mono, 8 g Poly, 2 g Sat); 0 mg Cholesterol; 67 g Carbohydrate (10 g Fibre, 43 g Sugar); 6 g Protein; 75 mg Sodium

Though still mild as far as greens go, Romaine lettuce has a slightly stronger flavour in a smoothie than spinach does. Green smoothie newbies might want to add a little more fruit if the flavour is too noticeable.

Apple Kiwi Kale

Kale has a strong distinct flavour that some people might find off-putting, but the nutrition this super green offers means it deserves a spot on everyone's plate (or in this case, smoothie). High in phytonutrients, kale is perhaps best known for its cancer-fighting properties, but it can also help stabilize blood sugar, lower blood pressure and reduce the risk of heart disease. In this smoothie, kale's rather bitter flavour is balanced by the sweet creaminess of the banana and the tanginess of kiwi.

Kiwi fruit, peeled	2	2
Frozen banana	1	1
Fresh kale leaves, stems removed	2 cups	500 mL
Apple juice	1 cup	250 mL
Ice cubes	8	8

Combine the first 4 ingredients in a blender until smooth. Add the ice and blend again until smooth and icy. Makes 2 servings.

1 serving: 200 Calories; 1.5 g Total Fat (0 g Mono, 0 g Poly, 0 g Sat); 0 mg Cholesterol; 48 g Carbohydrate (5 g Fibre, 29 g Sugar); 4 g Protein; 50 mg Sodium

Although people generally peel kiwi fruit before eating it, the skin is actually edible too. Most of the fibre and much of the vitamin C is found in the skin, so if you can get past the fuzzy texture, you're better off eating the fruit with the skin on.

Strawberry Carrot

We've probably all heard that eating carrots will give you good eyesight, and while that is not exactly true, carrots are an excellent source of beta-carotene, which the body converts into vitamin A and which is known to support eye health. Vitamin A helps protect the surface of the eye, is essential for night vision and may help prevent macular degeneration. If you have a powerful blender you can make this smoothie with raw carrots, but the texture will be unpleasant if your blender is not strong enough.

Frozen strawberries	1 cup	250 mL
Frozen banana	1	1
Chopped cooked carrot	2 cups	500 mL
Chia seeds	1 tbsp.	15 mL
Milk	3/4 cup	175 mL
Vanilla Greek yogurt	3/4 cup	175 mL
Maple syrup or honey	2 tsp.	10 mL

Combine all the ingredients in a blender until smooth. Makes 2 servings.

1 serving: 290 Calories; 3.5 g Total Fat (0 g Mono, 1 g Poly, 1.5 g Sat); 10 mg Cholesterol; 56 g Carbohydrate (6 g Fibre, 38 g Sugar); 14 g Protein; 170 mg Sodium

Though the carrot plant was already being cultivated as far back as the 8th century BC in Babylon, it was most likely grown for its leaves, as there is no evidence to suggest that carrots were part of the Babylonians' diet.

Green Chill

With its high protein content and wealth of micronutrients, spirulina is one of the most nutrient-dense foods you can include in your diet. However, it is algae, and as such has a distinct "oceany" taste that can be off-putting. There is not much you can do to mask the flavour, but pairing it with boldly flavoured fruit like pineapple and apple helps mellow the taste somewhat. It also helps to drink the smoothie when it is really cold, which makes your taste buds less sensitive.

Frozen pineapple chunks	1/2 cup	125 mL
Medium apple, cored and chopped	1/2 cup	125 mL
Baby spinach	1/2 cup	125 mL
Spirulina	1/2 tsp.	2 mL
Maple syrup or honey, to taste		
Vanilla almond milk	1 1/2 cups	375 mL
Apple juice	1/4 cup	60 mL
Ice cubes	4	4

Combine first 7 ingredients in a blender until smooth. Add the ice and blend again until smooth and icy. Makes 2 servings.

1 serving: *170 Calories; 3 g Total Fat (1 g Mono, 1.5 g Poly, 0 g Sat); 0 mg Cholesterol; 30 g Carbohydrate (3 g Fibre, 15 g Sugar); 6 g Protein; 260 mg Sodium*

Although spinach is high in iron and calcium, neither one is easily absorbed by the body. The oxalic acid in spinach combines with the iron and calcium, reducing their bioavailability. To get the most out of your spinach, combine it with a good source of vitamin C, which will make the iron and calcium easier to absorb.

Berry Pepper Surprise

Peppers are members of the nightshade family, like the tomato and potato. They come in many colours, including green, yellow, orange, red and purple. Red sweet peppers are an excellent source of vitamin C and a good source of lycopene, which may protect heart health and help prevent several types of cancer, including stomach and lung cancer. The white membrane inside red peppers is edible, though most people cut it out along with the seeds, and is a good source of flavonoids. Chia gel makes this smoothie nice and thick without adding a lot of calories.

Frozen strawberries	1 cup	250 mL
Frozen red grapes (or cherries/blueberries)	1/2 cup	125 mL
Diced red bell pepper	1/2 cup	125 mL
Chia gel	1 cup	250 mL
Pomegranate berry juice	1 cup	250 mL
Water	1/2 cup	125 mL

Combine all the ingredients in a blender until smooth. Makes 2 servings.

1 serving: 180 Calories; 3.5 g Total Fat (0 g Mono, 2 g Poly, 0 g Sat); 0 mg Cholesterol; 38 g Carbohydrate (6 g Fibre, 29 g Sugar); 3 g Protein; 15 mg Sodium

To make chia gel, combine 2 tbsp. (30 mL) of chia seeds and 1 cup (250 mL) of water in a sealable container, like a mason jar. Let stand for 15 minutes, then give the jar a good shake to break up any clumps. Let stand for another 15 minutes, and it will be ready to use. Chia gel will keep, refrigerated, for about a week.

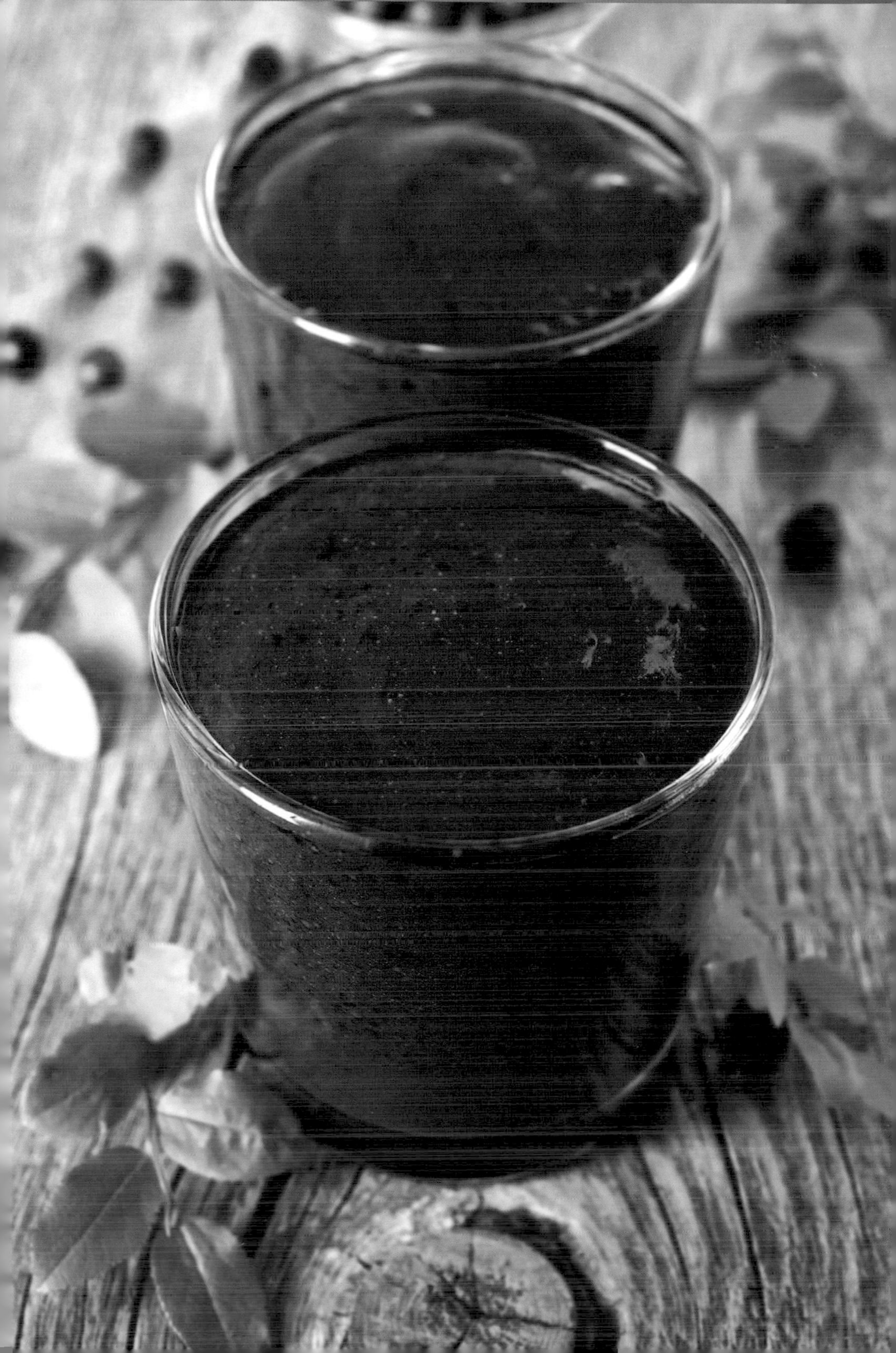

Gettin' Figgy with It

Next time you buy a bunch of fresh beets at the market, don't throw the greens into the compost; toss them into a smoothie instead. Not enough can be said about the importance of leafy greens in a healthy diet, and beet greens are a great addition. A good source of antioxidants, protein and fibre, beet greens are one of the milder-tasting greens, slightly more bitter than spinach but less than Swiss chard. In this smoothie, the figs' natural sweetness smooths out the flavour of the beet greens while adding another healthy dose of fibre as well as calcium and potassium.

Frozen pineapple	1 cup	250 mL
Chopped fresh figs, stems removed	1 1/2 cups	375 mL
Fresh or frozen red grapes	1 cup	250 mL
Chopped beet greens	1 cup	250 mL
Coconut water	1 1/2 cups	375 mL

Combine all the ingredients in a blender until smooth. Makes 2 servings.

1 serving: 320 Calories; 1 g Total Fat (0 g Mono, 0 g Poly, 0 g Sat); 0 mg Cholesterol; 87 g Carbohydrate (12 g Fibre, 66 g Sugar); 5 g Protein; 240 mg Sodium

The caprifig, the original wild fig from which cultivated figs are descended, can only be pollinated by the fig wasp, a gnat-sized wasp that crawls into the fig to lay her eggs, getting covered with pollen from the male flowers as she does so.

Cucumber Melon

Honeydew melon contains a chemical called adenosine, a type of anticoagulant that can reduce the risk of strokes or heart disease by preventing blood clots from forming. It is also an excellent source of vitamin C and potassium, and a good source of folate. With Swiss chard we are getting into the stronger-tasting greens, but its flavour blends well with the banana and melon. Cucumber makes this smoothie extra hydrating.

Honeydew melon, cubed	2 cups	500 mL
Frozen banana	1	1
Swiss chard	1 cup	250 mL
Peeled, chopped cucumber	1 cup	250 mL
Fresh mint leaves	6	6
Lime juice	1 tsp.	5 mL
Coconut water	1 cup	250 mL

Combine all the ingredients in a blender until smooth. Makes 2 servings.

1 serving: 150 Calories; 0.5 g Total Fat (0 g Mono, 0 g Poly, 0 g Sat); 0 mg Cholesterol; 36 g Carbohydrate (5 g Fibre, 25 g Sugar); 3 g Protein; 200 mg Sodium

Cucumber skin is an excellent source of chlorophyll, but include it in your smoothie only if it has no wax on it. If you have questionable faith in the power of your blender, opt for English cucumber or mini cucumbers, which have the fewest seeds.

Strawberry Pineapple Pea

Though we tend to think of them as vegetables, peas are actually a type of legume. As such, they are an excellent source of protein and fibre. They are also rich in antioxidants and contain coumestrol, a polyphenol that is thought to prevent stomach cancer. In smoothies, fresh or frozen peas act as a thickener, making the smoothie creamy without adding a lot of fat. If you don't have fresh pineapple on hand, you could substitute frozen, but you'll need to add more liquid to blend it.

Frozen strawberries	2 cups	500 mL
Fresh pineapple	1 cup	250 mL
Frozen peas	1/2 cup	125 mL
Ground flaxseed	1 tbsp.	15 mL
Coconut water	1 cup	250 mL

Combine all the ingredients in a blender until smooth. Makes 2 servings.

1 serving: 160 Calories; 2.5 g Total Fat (0 g Mono, 1.5 g Poly, 0 g Sat); 0 mg Cholesterol; 32 g Carbohydrate (8 g Fibre, 19 g Sugar); 5 g Protein; 170 mg Sodium

To get the full nutritional benefits of flaxseed, it must be ground before being added to your food. Whole flaxseeds will simply pass through the body undigested. You can purcha___ ground flax, but you'd be b___ ___inding the seeds ___ ___e grinder. Not only ___ ___al in the long run, ___ ___tritious. When ___osed to oxygen, which makes its polyunsaturated fats ___t by the time you eat it, the flaxseed has lost some of

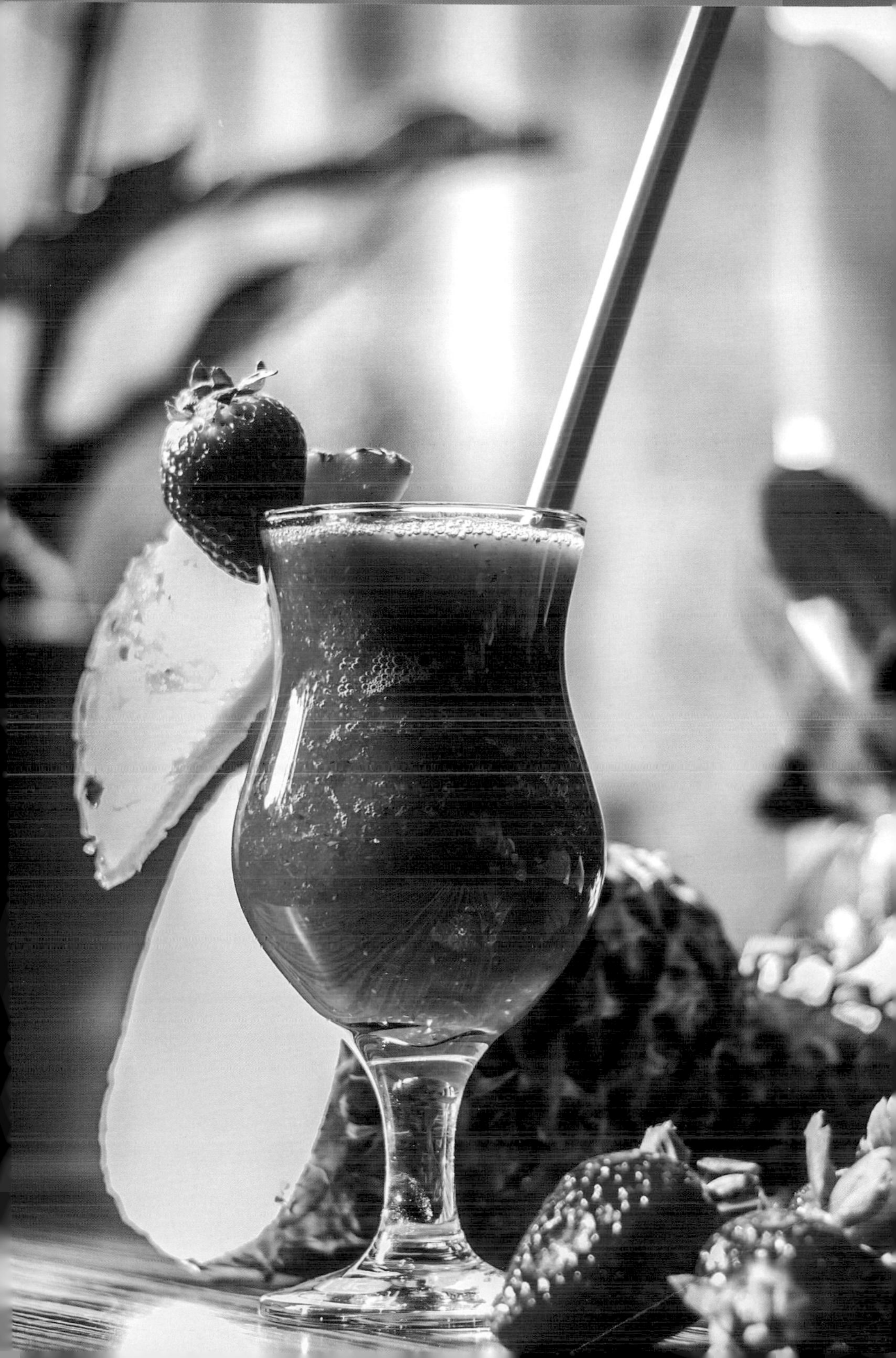

Mango Berry Spinach

The best thing about frozen fruit is that it allows you to make delicious smoothies like this one year round! There is so much going on in this smoothie that it is filling enough to be a full meal replacement. The sweetness of the dates, mango and grapes complements the tartness of the cherries and blackberries. Pecans add a little protein, but you could always toss in a spoonful of hemp seeds or chia seeds if you'd like a little more. A full cup of spinach may sound like a lot, but you won't even notice it with all the berries.

Frozen mango	1 cup	250 mL
Frozen cherries	1 cup	250 mL
Frozen blackberries	3/4 cup	175 mL
Frozen red grapes	1/2 cup	125 mL
Dates	4	4
Pecans	1/4 cup	60 mL
Baby spinach	1 cup	250 mL
Vanilla extract	1 tsp.	5 mL
Almond milk	2 cups	500 mL

Combine all the ingredients in a blender until smooth. Makes 2 servings.

1 serving: 410 Calories; 13 g Total Fat (6 g Mono, 3 g Poly, 1 g Sat); 0 mg Cholesterol; 74 g Carbohydrate (12 g Fibre, 57 g Sugar); 6 g Protein; 170 mg Sodium

Frozen grapes are more than just a tasty snack. They are a great addition to smoothies, adding a touch of sweetness without resorting to refined sugars and giving the smoothie a frosty texture.

Apple Pea Green Smoothie

   This is a mild-tasting green smoothie, perfect for those who are new to adding vegetables to their drinks. Green peas have a mild but distinctive flavour that pairs perfectly with apple. As you get accustomed to their flavour in a smoothie, try increasing the amount up to a full cup (250 mL). With the frozen peas and banana, this smoothie is quite thick; feel free to thin it out with a little apple juice or water, if need be. The fresh mint is optional, but it adds a whole different level of flavour to this smoothie.

Frozen peas	1/2 cup	125 mL
Frozen banana	1	1
Medium apple, chopped	1	1
Baby spinach	1 cup	250 mL
Almond butter	1 tbsp.	15 mL
Hemp seed	1 tbsp.	15 mL
Fresh mint, optional	1 tsp.	5 mL
Apple juice or coconut water, optional		

Combine all the ingredients in a blender until smooth. Makes 2 servings.

1 serving: 220 Calories; 7 g Total Fat (1 g Mono, 0 g Poly, 0 g Sat); 0 mg Cholesterol; 37 g Carbohydrate (7 g Fibre, 22 g Sugar); 7 g Protein; 105 mg Sodium

Pea plants are nitrogen-fixing plants, meaning that they take nitrogen from the air and add it to the soil in a form that is usable by other plants. Basically, growing pea plants enriches the soil without the need for added fertilizers. So not only are peas good for our health, but they are good for the environment, too!

Broccoli Acai

    Although broccoli has a rather strong flavour, it is barely noticeable in this smoothie, thanks to the rich flavours of the blueberry and acai. As part of the brassica family, broccoli has a wealth of health benefits and cancer-fighting properties, and it is also a good source of calcium. As with spinach, the calcium in broccoli is hard for the body to absorb, but combining it with vitamin C–rich blueberries and acai increases its bioavailability.

Frozen broccoli florets	2 cups	500 mL
Frozen blueberries	1 cup	250 mL
Frozen banana	1	1
Almonds	1/4 cup	60 mL
Acai powder	3 tbsp.	45 mL
Water	2 cups	500 mL
Maple syrup or honey, to taste		

Combine all the ingredients in a blender until smooth. Makes 2 servings.

1 serving: 320 Calories; 14 g Total Fat (6 g Mono, 2.5 g Poly, 3 g Sat); 0 mg Cholesterol; 41 g Carbohydrate (7 g Fibre, 20 g Sugar); 10 g Protein; 50 mg Sodium

Almonds are a good source of calcium, and they are high in potassium and monounsaturated fat, which helps protect heart health.

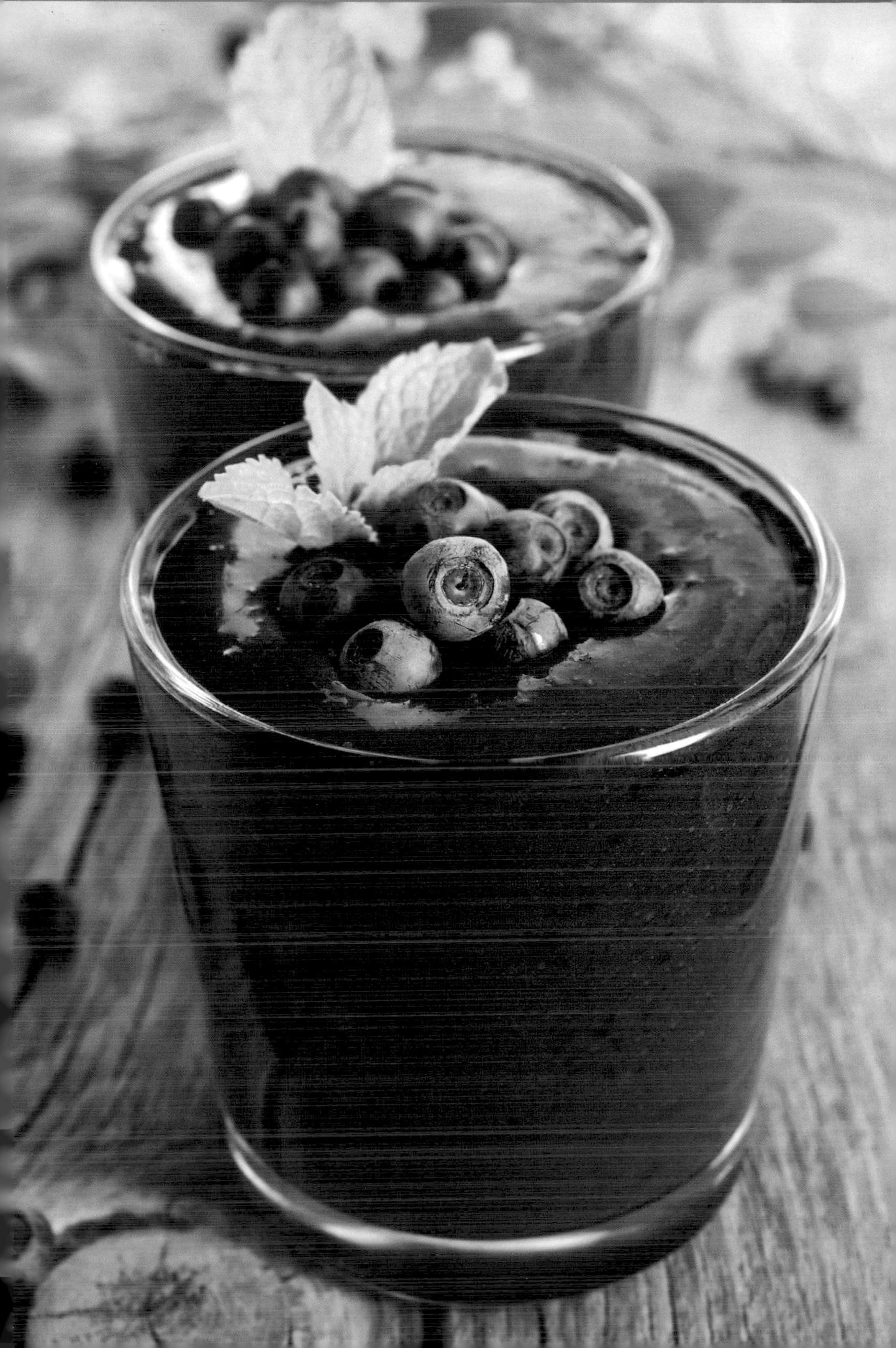

Sweeteners

In the interest of keeping smoothies healthy, we don't like to add refined sugar. For most recipes, the fresh or frozen fruit adds enough sweetness, particularly if you are using banana, pineapple and strawberries. There are times, though, when a touch of extra sweetness can make all the difference. It is not enough to make smoothies that are healthy for you; they have to taste great, too. No one wants to choke down a glassful of unpalatable blend, no matter how beneficial it may be. So if your smoothie is a bit lacklustre and would benefit from a little extra sweetness, don't feel bad about adding a little in. Just try to choose a healthier option. Sometimes a good splash of 100 percent fruit juice will do the trick, but if not, the following are a few of our favourite sweeteners.

Dried fruit: dates, raisins and apricots are all good bets. They add natural sugar as well as concentrated nutrition. Dates and raisins are high in iron, and apricots are a good source of calcium.

Coconut sugar: relatively new to supermarket shelves, coconut sugar has been cited as a "best choice" sweetener because it contains trace amounts of vitamins, minerals and antioxidants and is less processed than refined white sugar. It is also lower on the glycemic index (a rating system that measures how quickly foods raise blood sugar levels), meaning that it does not cause the spike in blood sugar that white sugar causes. An added benefit is that coconut sugar is more environmentally friendly than any other sweetener; in 2014, UN's Food and Agriculture Organization declared it the most sustainable type of sweetener worldwide. Coconut palms require less water to grow than sugar cane plants and yield more of the finished product, and coconut sugar is not chemically altered in any way, resulting in a smaller ecological footprint.

Maple syrup: boiled down from the sap of the sugar maple, this syrup has surprising nutritional benefits considering that it is essentially just sugar. Maple syrup has anti-inflammatory properties, is a good source of antioxidants and is high in zinc, riboflavin and manganese (just 1 tbsp., 15 mL, contains 25 percent of the daily recommended intake for this important mineral). It is also lower on the glycemic index than refined white sugar, about the same as honey or molasses.

Honey: one of the oldest known sweeteners, honey has been used since at least the time of the ancient Egyptians. In its raw form, honey is taken directly from the hive and bottled; pasteurized honey has been treated to kill any yeast cells that might have been lurking in the nectar that went on to become the honey. The composition of honey depends on what kind of flowers the bee visited, but honey contains trace amounts of the minerals, vitamins and proteins found in the original plant. Eating local raw honey may help allergy sufferers build up a resistance to the plants in their vicinity. Honey is also believed to provide a measure of relief from colds, acting as a natural cough suppressant.

Date syrup: also known as date molasses, this natural sweetener has a long history of use in Middle Eastern cooking. It is made by boiling down dates until they are reduced to a thick syrup, about the same consistency as honey. Because it is minimally processed, date syrup still contains much of the nutrients found in dates, and it is on the low end of the glycemic index, so it does not cause the quick spike in blood sugar levels that refined white sugar is known for.

Stevia: this natural sweetener is extracted from the leaves of the stevia plant, which grows in South America. Stevia seems to be a "love it or hate it" product. Some people swear by stevia and add it to everything in place of sugar, whereas others cannot get past the taste. Stevia is extremely sweet, about 200 to 300 times as sweet as sugar depending on the brand, and it does have a distinctive taste. Used sparingly, it can be an excellent sweetener; because it is calorie and carbohydrate free, it has no effect on blood sugar, but if you add too much, it can leave a bitter aftertaste. Stevia comes in both a liquid and powdered form; the liquid form works best in smoothies because it is easier to control how much you are adding. A drop or two in the mix is all you'll need.

Sinless Mocha Frappe

While it may be a stretch to call this smoothie healthy, it is at least a healthier alternative to the overpriced, sugar-laden frappes you'd buy from your local coffee shop. We've used cacao in place of chocolate syrup and coconut sugar in place of refined white sugar. Coconut sugar is lower on the glycemic index than regular sugar, which means it does not cause your blood sugar and insulin levels to spike the way regular sugar does. For a truly decadent drink, top with whipped cream and a sprinkle of cacao nibs or some shavings of dark chocolate.

Cold brewed coffee	1 1/2 cups	375 mL
Unsweetened almond milk	1/2 cup	125 mL
Vanilla extract	1 tsp.	5 mL
Cacao	2 tbsp.	30 mL
Coconut sugar	1 tsp.	5 mL
Ice cubes	12	12

Combine the first 5 ingredients in a blender until smooth. Add the ice and blend again until smooth and icy. Makes 2 servings.

1 serving: 50 Calories; 2 g Total Fat (0.5 g Mono, 0.5 g Poly, 0.5 g Sat); 0 mg Cholesterol; 6 g Carbohydrate (3 g Fibre, 3 g Sugar); 3 g Protein; 10 mg Sodium

To make cold brewed coffee, place 1 cup (250 mL) coursely ground coffee beans in a large bowl. Stir in 4 cups (1L) water and refrigerate, covered, for 12 to 24 hours. Line a fine-mesh strainer with cheesecloth and place over another large bowl or pitcher. Pour the coffee slowly through the strainer, filtering out the grounds. Discard the grounds and refrigerate the coffee, covered, for up to 7 days. Makes 4 cups (1 L).

Chocolate Quinoa Cooler

Over the last few years, quinoa has gained superfood status. It is one of the few plant foods that is a source of complete protein, meaning that it contains all the essential amino acids, and it is also a good source of fibre, minerals and vitamins B and E, to name a few. Thanks to its fibre and high quality protein, quinoa fills you up fast. The combination of dates, quinoa and cacao powder makes for an extremely rich, satisfying smoothie. A little goes a long way.

Dates	5	5
Cooked quinoa	1/2 cup	125 mL
Cacao powder	1/2 cup	125 mL
Cacao nibs	1 tsp.	5 mL
Coconut sugar	1 tsp.	5 mL
Almond milk	1 cup	250 mL
Vanilla extract	1 tsp.	5 mL
Ice cubes	8	8

Combine the first 7 ingredients in a blender until smooth. Add the ice and blend again until smooth and icy. Makes 2 servings.

1 serving: 250 Calories; 7 g Total Fat (1.5 g Mono, 1.5 g Poly, 2.5 g Sat); 0 mg Cholesterol; 48 g Carbohydrate (11 g Fibre, 21 g Sugar); 16 g Protein; 60 mg Sodium

Coconut sugar is not made from coconuts, as the name suggests. Rather, it is made by boiling down the sap of flower buds from the coconut palm tree until the water has evaporated.

Gingerbread Shake

A smoothie with the comforting aromas of fresh gingerbread. This smoothie has a rather mild, soothing flavour; feel free to add more ginger or molasses if you prefer a more boldly flavoured drink. Molasses is an excellent, if underused, sweetener. Unlike refined sugar, blackstrap molasses still has nutritional value. It is a good source of iron, copper, calcium, potassium and manganese. Blackstrap molasses has a strong, distinct flavour that some may find overpowering. If the flavour is too strong for your taste, choose a milder molasses. It will have less nutrients than blackstrap but is still a healthier choice than refined sugar. Just be sure to choose an unsulphured variety.

Raisins	1/2 cup	125 mL
Avocado	1/2	1/2
Grated ginger root	1/2 tsp.	2 mL
Ground cinnamon	1/2 tsp.	2 mL
Ground nutmeg, sprinkle		
Ground cloves, sprinkle		
Blackstrap molasses	1 tsp.	5 mL
Vanilla extract	1 tsp.	5 mL
Unsweetened vanilla almond milk	2 cups	500 mL
Ice cubes	8	8

Combine the first 9 ingredients in a blender until smooth. Add the ice and blend again until smooth and icy. Makes 2 servings.

1 serving: 580 Calories; 22 g Total Fat (11 g Mono, 6 g Poly, 3 g Sat); 0 mg Cholesterol; 84 g Carbohydrate (17 g Fibre, 63 g Sugar); 18 g Protein; 75 mg Sodium

The ginger plant, *Zingiber officinale*, is not known to grow in the wild, but it has been cultivated for centuries. It most likely originated in southern Asia.

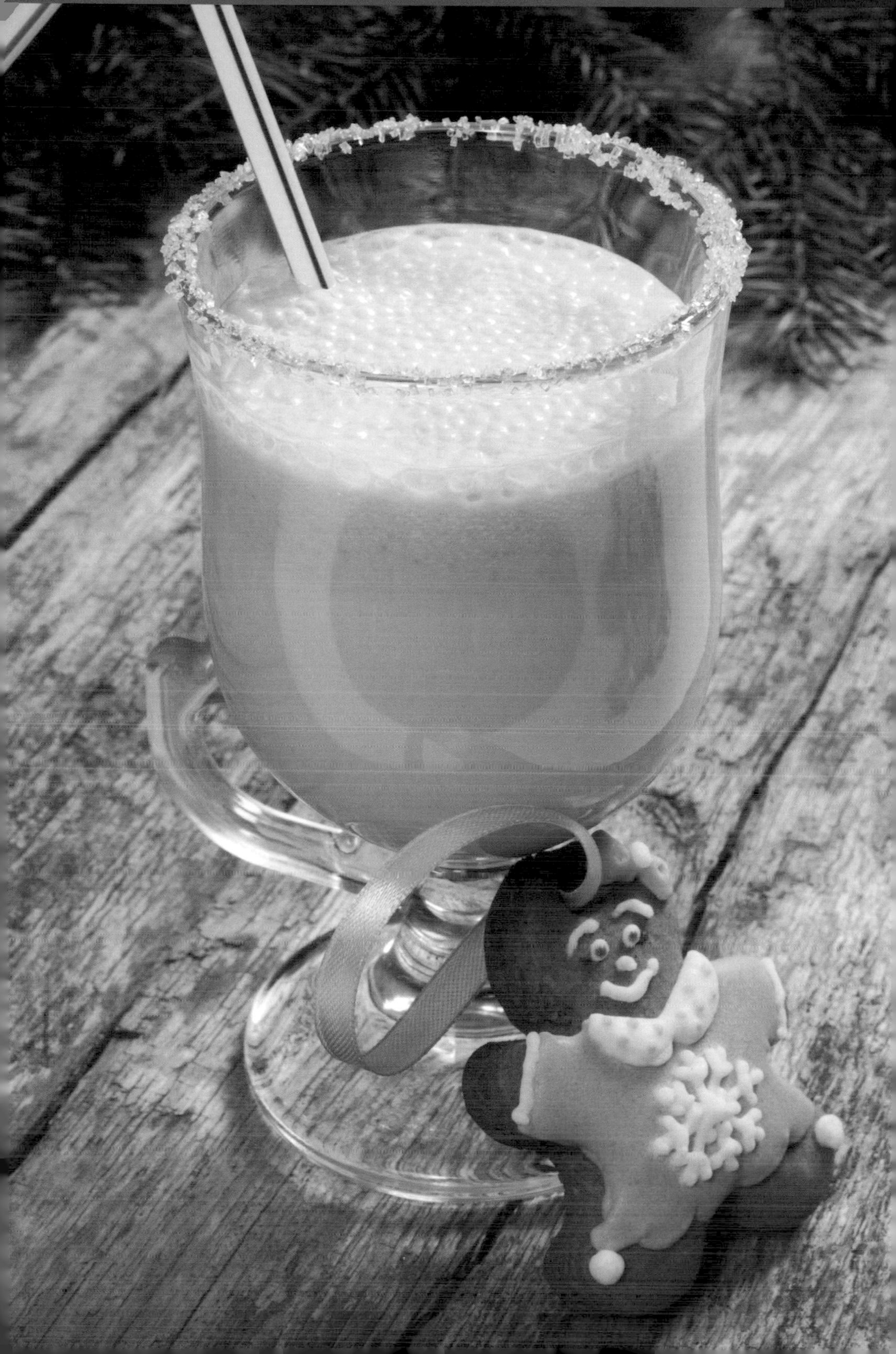

Frosty PB and J

   This smoothie has all the flavour of a peanut butter and jam sandwich with none of the mess. It is the perfect breakfast to take on the go. Choose natural peanut butter to avoid the added sugar and hydrogenated oils found in the regular varieties. If strawberries are not your thing, replace them with your favourite berry. Raspberries are an especially tasty substitute.

Frozen banana	1	1
Frozen strawberries	1 cup	250 mL
Natural peanut butter	2 tbsp.	30 mL
Honey	1 tbsp.	15 mL
Milk	3/4 cup	175 mL
Ice cubes	8	8

Combine the first 5 ingredients in a blender until smooth. Add the ice and blend again until smooth and icy. Makes 2 servings.

1 serving: 250 Calories; 10 g Total Fat (0 g Mono, 0 g Poly, 2.5 g Sat); trace Cholesterol; 37 g Carbohydrate (4 g Fibre, 26 g Sugar); 9 g Protein; 135 mg Sodium

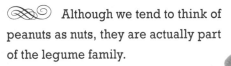 Although we tend to think of peanuts as nuts, they are actually part of the legume family.

Pumpkin Cheesecake In a Glass

Pumpkin doesn't have to be relegated to autumn with this delicious smoothie. Canned pumpkin makes this recipe easy and convenient to prepare, allowing you to take full advantage of pumpkin's health benefits with almost no effort. A 1 cup (250 mL) serving of mashed pumpkin provides more than 200 percent of the recommended daily intake of vitamin A, so necessary for healthy vision. It is also loaded with fibre, potassium and vitamin C. The banana and cream cheese make this smoothie ultra-creamy. Sweeten with a little honey, if necessary.

Frozen banana	1	1
Dates	4	4
Pecans	1/4 cup	60 mL
Canned pumpkin	1 1/2 cups	375 mL
Cream cheese	1/4 cup	60 mL
Ground cinnamon	1/2 tsp.	2 mL
Ground nutmeg, sprinkle		
Ground allspice, sprinkle		
Vanilla extract	1 tsp.	5 mL
Unsweetened vanilla almond milk	1 cup	250 mL
Ice cubes	8	8

Combine the first 10 ingredients in a blender until smooth. Add the ice and blend again until smooth and icy. Makes 2 servings.

1 serving: 400 Calories; 22 g Total Fat (6 g Mono, 4 g Poly, 6 g Sat); 35 mg Cholesterol; 47 g Carbohydrate (13 g Fibre, 27 g Sugar); 12 g Protein; 150 mg Sodium

Although its origins are unclear, cheesecake dates back to at least the days of ancient Rome. A description of it appears in Roman text dating back to the 2nd century BC.

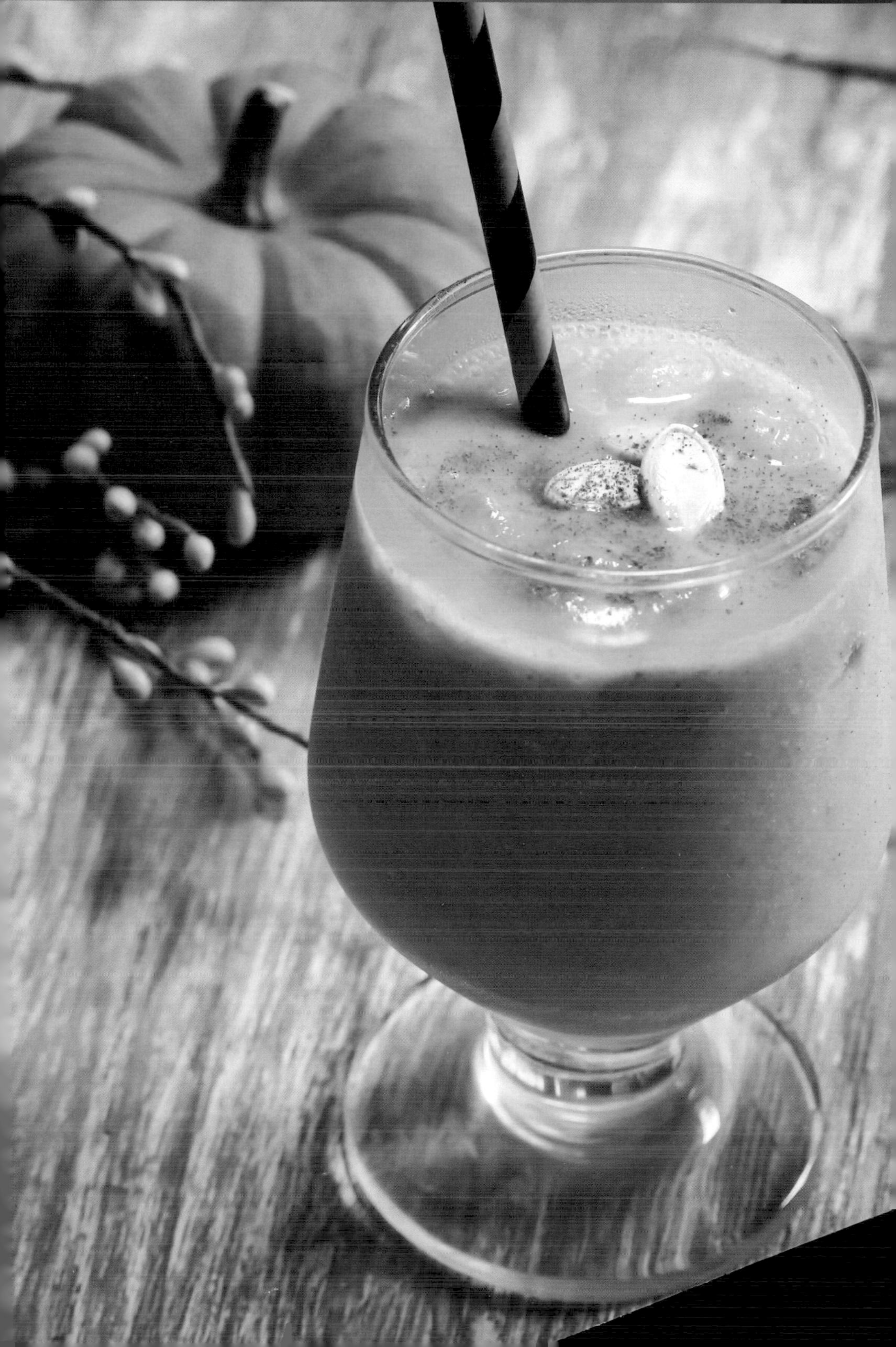

Cookies 'n' Cream Chiller

  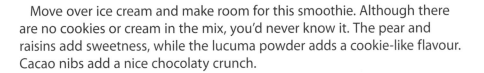

Move over ice cream and make room for this smoothie. Although there are no cookies or cream in the mix, you'd never know it. The pear and raisins add sweetness, while the lucuma powder adds a cookie-like flavour. Cacao nibs add a nice chocolaty crunch.

Raisins	1/4 cup	60 mL
Pecans	1/4 cup	60 mL
Cacao nibs	2 tbsp.	30 mL
Fresh ripe pear, chopped	1	1
Lucuma powder	2 tbsp.	30 mL
Almond-coconut milk	1 1/2 cups	375 mL
Ice cubes	16	16

Combine the first 6 ingredients in a blender until smooth. Add the ice and blend again until smooth and icy. Makes 2 servings.

1 serving: 340 Calories; 17 g Total Fat (6 g Mono, 3 g Poly, 7 g Sat); 0 mg Cholesterol; 42 g Carbohydrate (11 g Fibre, 27 g Sugar); 4 g Protein; 85 mg Sodium

If you are not avoiding dairy, you could substitute milk for the almond-coconut milk to make this treat taste even more like ice cream.

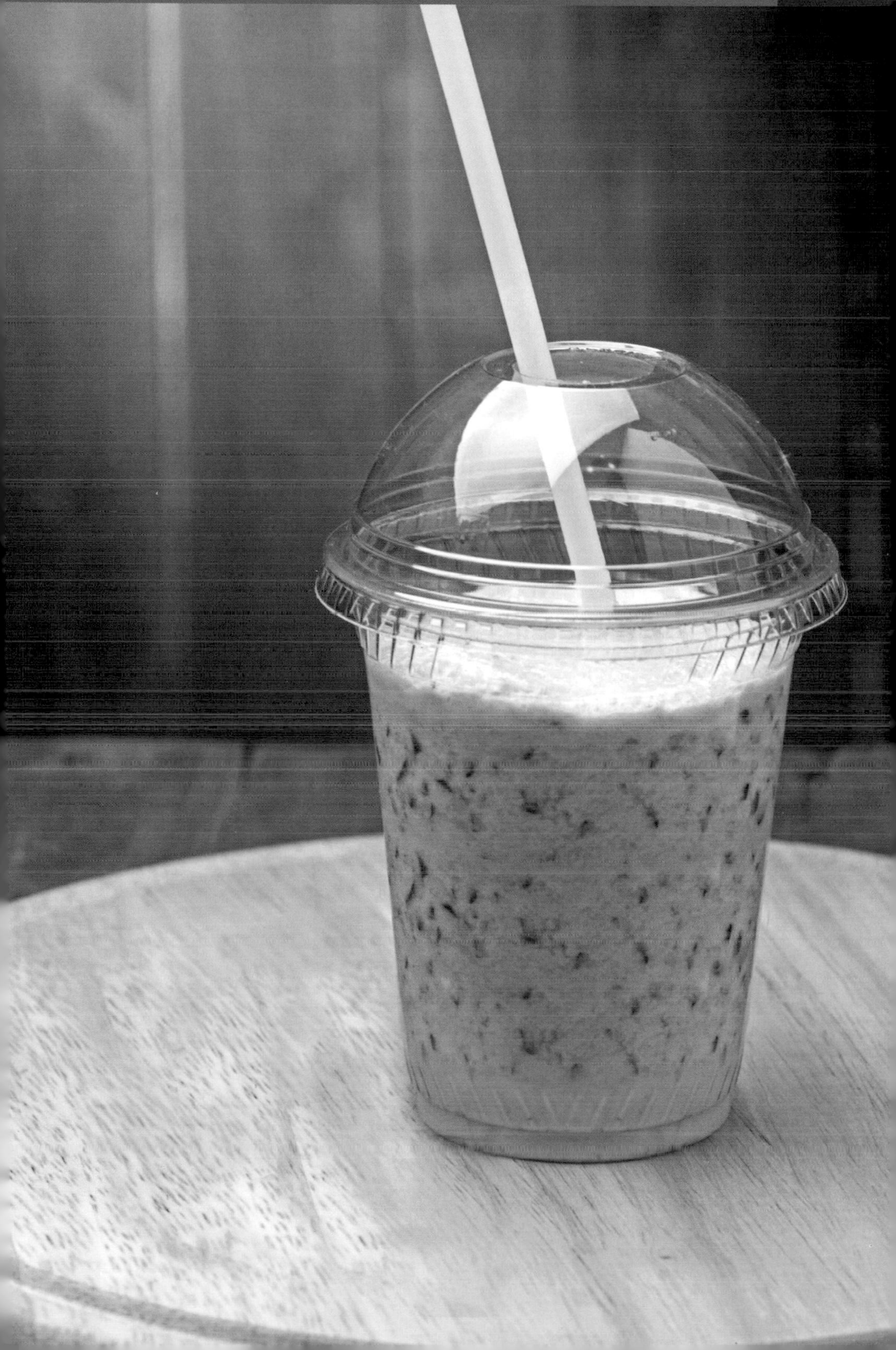

Icy Apple Pie

Not all healthy smoothies have to be meal replacements; some can be pure indulgence. Curb that craving for apple pie with this delicious smoothie. The dates and lucuma powder add sweetness without refined sugar, while the Greek yogurt makes the smoothie rich and creamy without a lot of added fat.

Medium apples, cored and chopped	2	2
Dates	4	4
Ground cinnamon	1 tsp.	5 mL
Ground nutmeg, sprinkle		
Ginger, sprinkle		
Lucuma powder	1 tbsp.	15 mL
Ground flaxseed	1 tbsp.	15 mL
Vanilla Greek yogurt	1/2 cup	125 mL
Unsweetened almond milk	2 cups	500 mL
Ice cubes	8	8

Combine the first 9 ingredients in a blender until smooth. Add the ice and blend again until smooth and icy. Makes 2 servings.

1 serving: 350 Calories; 7 g Total Fat (1.5 g Mono, 4.5 g Poly, 1.5 g Sat); 5 mg Cholesterol; 59 g Carbohydrate (9 g Fibre, 42 g Sugar); 14 g Protein; 120 mg Sodium

Although it had been grown on a small scale in Canada since the early 1600s, flax didn't become an important crop until immigrant farmers settling the prairies in the 1800s introduced it to their gardens. Today, Saskatchewan and Manitoba are the largest flax producers in the country, and they grow almost half of the world's flax crop.

Cinnamon Bun Smoothie

Another perfect breakfast smoothie! Start the day off right with this healthy drink that has all the flavours of a cinnamon bun without any of the empty calories or guilt. This smoothie has more fat than a lot of the other offerings in the book, but it is heart healthy fat from the almond butter and avocado. Feel free to add a little extra cinnamon, if you'd like.

Dates	4	4
Almond butter	1 tsp.	5 mL
Avocado	1/2	1/2
Toasted wheat germ	1/2 cup	125 mL
Chia seeds	1 tbsp.	15 mL
Vanilla Greek yogurt	1/2 cup	125 mL
Unsweetened vanilla almond milk	1 cup	250 mL
Vanilla extract	1 tsp.	5 mL
Ground cinnamon	1/2 tsp.	2 mL
Ice cubes	8	8

Combine the first 9 ingredients in a blender until smooth. Add the ice and blend again until smooth and icy. Makes 2 servings.

1 serving: 430 Calories; 24 g Total Fat (6 g Mono, 5 g Poly, 6 g Sat); 15 mg Cholesterol; 41 g Carbohydrate (14 g Fibre, 17 g Sugar); 19 g Protein; 55 mg Sodium

Not only does the toasted wheat germ give the smoothie mild nutty undertones, but it also adds calcium, iron, protein, antioxidants and many of the B vitamins, including folate and niacin.

Carrot Cake Shake

People often make the mistake of thinking that because it contains carrots, carrot cake must be healthy. Not true. Most carrot cakes are loaded with refined sugar and fat. This smoothie has all the flavour of your favourite carrot cake but is loaded with ingredients that support your health, not undermine it. The carrots add a lot of sweetness, but if you need a little more, add a splash of maple syrup or honey. Add a little ice if you like it really frosty.

Frozen mango	1 cup	250 mL
Walnuts	1/4 cup	60 mL
Cooked chopped carrot	2 cups	500 mL
Vanilla Greek yogurt	1/2 cup	125 mL
Hemp seeds	1 tbsp.	15 mL
Ground cinnamon	1/2 tsp.	2 mL
Nutmeg, sprinkle		
Unsweetened almond milk	1 cup	250 mL
Vanilla extract	1 tsp.	5 mL

Combine all the ingredients in a blender until smooth. Makes 2 servings.

1 serving: 360 Calories; 20 g Total Fat (2.5 g Mono, 9 g Poly, 5 g Sat); 15 mg Cholesterol; 36 g Carbohydrate (9 g Fibre, 22 g Sugar); 12 g Protein; 140 mg Sodium

Nutmeg contains a substance called myristicin, which has a narcotic effect when consumed in large quantities.

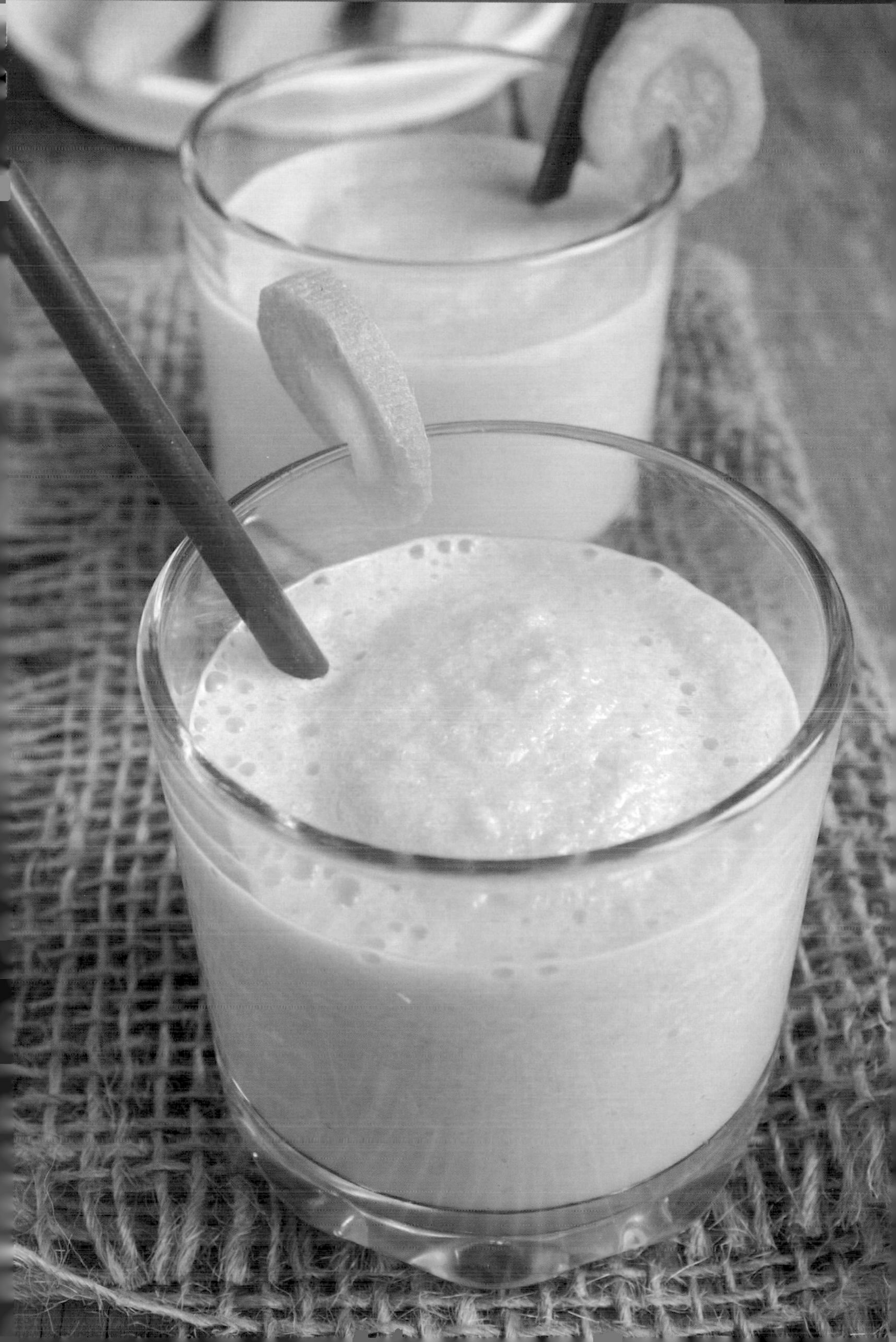

Juicing

Juicing has become a popular way of adding extra vitamins and essential nutrients to the diet amidst an array of increasingly processed foods at grocery stores. Processed foods often lack many vitamins and minerals, and while it's difficult not to eat any processed foods, we can easily compensate by also juicing with superfoods. Juicing at home is superior to buying juices in the store, as many micronutrients are quite sensitive and become damaged or destroyed when juice is pasteurized. Whenever possible, choose organic produce to juice. The skin of fruits and vegetables often contains most of their minerals, so juicing them whole is the best way to maximize mineral and vitamin extraction. All fresh juices are prone to rapid oxidation, so drink the juice as soon as you make it. Clean the juicer afterwards, not before you enjoy the juice.

Although results will vary between individuals, some of the benefits of juicing with superfoods may include increased energy, reduced stress, increased ability to handle stress, weight reduction, and improved memory and brain function. Combined with other healthy lifestyle and diet choices, as well as good sleep practices, juicing is an ideal way to supercharge your immune system and maximize your productivity.

Hearty Anti-Inflammatory

This hearty juice is well named; several of the ingredients support heart and circulatory health. Grapefruit has properties that help prevent heart disease, but it can interfere with how the body metabolizes some medications, so if you are taking any heart medication, omit the grapefruit from this recipe or substitute orange or lemon. Burdock root is a powerful blood cleanser and has notable anti-inflammatory properties. It is best used fresh but can be hard to find. Try local Asian food stores or farmers' markets. Be sure to juice the burdock last as it oxidizes quickly.

Purple cabbage	1 cup	250 mL
Beet	1	1
Celery stalks	2	2
Fresh ripe pear	1	1
Grapefruit, peeled	1/2	1/2
Burdock root (about 3 inches, 7.5 cm, long)	1	1

Juice all the ingredients in the order given and stir lightly. Makes 1 serving.

1 serving: 190 Calories; 0 g Total Fat (0 g Mono, 0 g Poly, 0 g Sat); 0 mg Cholesterol; 60 g Carbohydrate (14 g Fibre, 37 g Sugar); 5 g Protein; 160 mg Sodium

Purple cabbage provides all the benefits of other cruciferous vegetables, but its colour makes for a prettier juice!

Skin Tonic

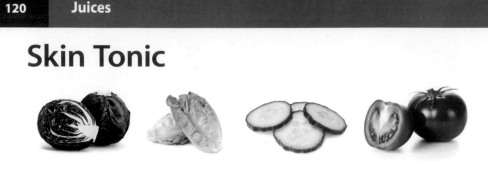

Extreme juicers often juice several bunches of green leafy vegetables per day. This juice introduces a large amount of leaf in a very palatable way. Romaine lettuce has a wonderful colour and mild, grassy flavour. Cucumber provides nutrients essential for skin and hair health, while tomatoes and a dash of salt impart the umami that is so often missing in juices. Salt also helps to disguise any bitterness from the greens.

Purple cabbage	2 cups	500 mL
Head of romaine lettuce	1	1
Medium cucumber	1	1
Tomatoes	2	2
Cayenne pepper, to taste		
Sea salt, sprinkle		

Juice the cabbage, lettuce, cucumber and tomatoes. Whisk in the cayenne pepper and salt. Makes 1 serving.

1 serving: 140 Calories; 0 g Total Fat (0 g Mono, 0 g Poly, 0 g Sat); 0 mg Cholesterol; 43 g Carbohydrate (10 g Fibre, 22 g Sugar); 10 g Protein; 220 mg Sodium

Umami is one of the five basic tastes, along with bitterness, saltiness, sweetness and sourness. Umami is best described as savouriness. Tomatoes and some fermented vegetables can impart this delicious flavour.

Gingerade

This simple juice is often paired with meals in India. The ginger and lemon together are hydrating and energizing. Because ginger requires a juicer while lemons can just be squeezed, a good time-saving tip is to juice a large quantity of ginger at one time and freeze the juice in ice cube trays. Add one cube to your fresh-squeezed lemonade. This trick works well with ginger but not with other juices because ginger juice oxidizes less than the juice of other vegetables.

Lemons	2	2
Ginger root (1 inch, 2.5 cm, piece)	1	1
Water	2 cups	500 mL
Agave syrup or honey, to taste		

Juice the lemons with a squeezer, or peel and put through the juicer with the ginger. Whisk in the agave syrup or honey. Makes 1 serving.

1 serving: 50 Calories; 0 g Total Fat (0 g Mono, 0 g Poly, 0 g Sat); 0 mg Cholesterol; 18 g Carbohydrate (3 g Fibre, 3 g Sugar); 1 g Protein; 0 mg Sodium

If you prefer lemonade over gingerade, replace the ginger root with 3 sprigs of fresh mint.

Classic Morning Energizer

Celery is an excellent addition to any morning juice. It hydrates the body with well-balanced electrolytes—a great start to any day! Beet and carrots provide a wealth of antioxidants and vitamins, especially beta-carotene. Grapefruit brings in the familiar flavour of a country breakfast, while ginger adds the zest that wakes you up and energizes you for the rest of the day.

Celery stalks	2	2
Beet	1	1
Medium carrots	4	4
Grapefruit, peeled	1/2	1/2
Ginger root (1 inch, 2.5 cm, piece)	1	1

Juice all the ingredients and stir lightly. Makes 1 serving.

1 serving: 160 Calories; 0 g Total Fat (0 g Mono, 0 g Poly, 0 g Sat); 0 mg Cholesterol; 48 g Carbohydrate (9 g Fibre, 28 g Sugar); 5 g Protein; 300 mg Sodium

Ginger root is rich in minerals and vitamins, and drinking the juice helps to combat fatigue, inflammation, nausea and digestive disorders.

Bright and Light Quench

The combination of fennel and celery in this refreshing juice brings the hydrating electrolytes of celery together with the digestion-calming effects of fennel. The sweet licorice flavour of the fennel pairs nicely with the orange and carrot—both of which are full of powerful antioxidants and vitamins to boost the immune system.

Medium oranges	4	4
Lemon	1	1
Carrots	3	3
Celery stalks	2	2
Fennel bulb	1/2	1/2

Juice the oranges and lemon with a squeezer, or peel and put through the juicer with the remaining ingredients. Makes 1 serving.

1 serving: 300 Calories; 1.5 g Total Fat (0 g Mono, 0 g Poly, 0 g Sat); 0 mg Cholesterol; 95 g Carbohydrate (24 g Fibre, 65 g Sugar); 9 g Protein; 250 mg Sodium

Fennel contains a phytonutrient called anethole, known to reduce inflammation and help prevent cancer. Fennel is also a good source of potassium, a valuable mineral that slashes your risk of heart disease, high blood pressure and stroke.

Vitamin C Crush

You'll fall in love with this vitamin C–rich juice that looks beautiful in your glass. Cranberries add a tart, wild flavour and impart many health benefits; cranberry juice is famous for supporting kidney and urinary tract health. The sprinkle of cardamom powder brings a warming flavour and adds several essential volatile oils and minerals.

Fresh strawberries	2 cups	500 mL
Carrots	2	2
Cantaloupe	1 cup	250 mL
Fresh cranberries	1/4 cup	60 mL
Ground cardamom, sprinkle		

Juice the strawberries, carrots, cantaloupe and cranberries. Whisk in the cardamom. Makes 1 serving.

1 serving: 160 Calories; 2 g Total Fat (0 g Mono, 0 g Poly, 0 g Sat); 0 mg Cholesterol; 50 g Carbohydrate (10 g Fibre, 33 g Sugar); 5 g Protein; 110 mg Sodium

Although cantaloupe ranks lower than other "superfoods" for most phytonutrients, studies have shown that eating good quantities of this fruit can decrease the risk of metabolic syndrome.

Summer Sunrise

Often overlooked by juicers, the skins of the noble grape are an excellent source of antioxidants. Additionally, they are the source of an overwhelming number of health-supportive phytonutrients. Grapes are quite sweet, however, and adding too many can overpower the other flavours in the juice. Keep this in mind if you encounter an unpalatable juice elsewhere; adding a handful of grapes may rescue the recipe for you.

Pomegranate, seeds only	1	1
Red grapes	1/2 cup	125 mL
Carrots	2	2
Medium orange, peeled	1	1
Fresh ripe pear	1	1
Ginger root (1 inch, 2.5 cm, piece)	1	1

Juice all the ingredients and stir lightly. Makes 1 serving.

1 serving: 260 Calories; 2 g Total Fat (0 g Mono, 0 g Poly, 0 g Sat); 0 mg Cholesterol; 80 g Carbohydrate (16 g Fibre, 55 g Sugar); 5 g Protein; 90 mg Sodium

Pomegranate, too, is an excellent source of antioxidants, specifically punicalagins. These and other phytonutrients contribute to pomegranate's anti-inflammatory and anti-cancer properties.

Beet Zinger

If you're looking for a juice with flavour and zing, this is the one! It's a guaranteed pick-me-up, with an immune boost as well. Watercress is a lovely addition to juice, imparting a peppery flavour. Often thought of as a lettuce, watercress is actually in the cruciferous family (along with cabbage, collards, kale and broccoli), and its health benefits include powerful anti-cancer properties.

Beets	2	2
Ginger root (1 inch, 2.5 cm, piece)	1	1
Small hot chili pepper, seeds and stem removed	1	1
Medium green apples	2	2
Celery stalks	2	2
Garlic clove	1	1
Watercress	1 cup	250 mL

Juice all the ingredients and stir lightly. Makes 1 serving.

1 serving: 230 Calories; 0.5 g Total Fat (0 g Mono, 0 g Poly, 0 g Sat); 0 mg Cholesterol; 67 g Carbohydrate (10 g Fibre, 46 g Sugar); 6 g Protein; 210 mg Sodium

Although it is rare, consuming high quantities of watercress can cause symptoms similar to a bladder infection in some people, such as the "urge to go" and slight burning while urinating. This is not an infection, though, and the sensations pass quickly.

Spring Tonic

Long-regarded as nothing more than an annoying weed, the humble dandelion is now entering the ranks of the most powerful anti-cancer plants known. When juicing dandelion greens be careful to use them before they wilt. Pair them with spirulina and you've got a nutrient-packed juice that nourishes and heals.

Celery stalks	2	2
Medium green apple	1	1
Medium cucumber	1	1
Small zucchini	1	1
Green bell pepper, seeds and stem removed	1/2	1/2
Fresh young dandelion greens	4	4
Spirulina	1 tsp.	5 mL

Juice the first 6 ingredients Whisk in the spirulina. Makes 1 serving.

1 serving: 160 Calories; 0 g Total Fat (0 g Mono, 0 g Poly, 0 g Sat); 0 mg Cholesterol; 44 g Carbohydrate (7 g Fibre, 27 g Sugar); 5 g Protein; 110 mg Sodium

Instead of looking for a place to buy dandelions, you can pick your own from any grassy area where you are certain no chemicals have been sprayed.

Tonic Bite

   For the more adventurous juicer, the entire dandelion plant is an excellent addition. The root is considered the most active part of the plant in terms of anti-cancer properties. Lightly wash the root, but don't worry if some soil particles remain. Anecdotal research suggests that these soil particles are beneficial to the action of the dandelion. The ginger and radishes give this juice a little bite, while the apples soften and sweeten the aftertaste.

Young dandelion plant, roots and leaves	1	1
Red radishes	2	2
Celery stalk, with leaves	1	1
Watercress	1/2 cup	125 mL
Medium apples	2	2
Lemon, peeled	1/2	1/2
Ginger root (1 inch, 2.5 cm, piece)	1	1

Juice the entire young dandelion plant followed by the other ingredients. Stir lightly. Makes 1 serving.

1 serving: 210 Calories; 1 g Total Fat (0 g Mono, 0 g Poly, 0 g Sat); 0 mg Cholesterol; 59 g Carbohydrate (7 g Fibre, 41 g Sugar); 3 g Protein; 55 mg Sodium

   Canadian scientists have received grants for research into the cancer-killing properties of dandelion roots, and some of the products they've developed are in clinical trials.

Antioxidant Refresher

Blueberries, pomegranate and cherries—all celebrated for their rich antioxidant content—make this richly coloured juice a potent health booster. In summer, use as many backyard fruits as possible; apples, raspberries and plums are common in gardens. Homegrown fruit has two major benefits: it is organic if you don't use chemicals in your garden, and fruit picked ripe from the plant (rather than ripening in transit) has the highest content of nutrients, antioxidants and vitamins.

Pomegranate, seeds only	1	1
Cherries, pitted	1 cup	250 mL
Plum, pitted	1	1
Medium red apple	1	1
Blueberries	1/2 cup	125 mL
Raspberries	1/2 cup	125 mL

Juice all the ingredients. Apples can be juiced whole (without removing the core). Stir lightly. Makes 1 serving.

1 serving: 320 Calories; 2 g Total Fat (0 g Mono, 0 g Poly, 0 g Sat); 0 mg Cholesterol; 96 g Carbohydrate (18 g Fibre, 50 g Sugar); 2 g Protein; 5 mg Sodium

The slight sourness of pomegranate juice is from acidic tannins. Although once thought to be anti-nutrients, tannins do play an important health role. The tannins specific to pomegranate can help prevent and heal stomach ulcers.

Early Harvest

   This wonderful juice evokes feelings of warm summer days, even when made in mid-winter. Arguably, the ideal time to make this juice is late in the afternoon on a warm summer day with fruit from your own garden. Fruit warmed and ripened in the sun is at its nutrient—and flavour—peak. Rich in vitamin C and beta-carotene, stone fruits have been shown to ward off obesity-related diseases such as diabetes, metabolic syndrome and cardiovascular disease. Cardamom gives the juice a warming and aromatic twist.

Raspberries	**1 cup**	**250 mL**
Nectarine, pitted	1	1
Apricots, pitted	2	2
Peach, pitted	1	1
Plums, pitted	2	2
Ground cardamom, to taste, optional		

Juice the first 5 ingredients and stir lightly. Whisk in cardamom, if using. Makes 1 serving.

1 serving: 210 Calories; 2 g Total Fat (0 g Mono, 0 g Poly, 0 g Sat); 0 mg Cholesterol; 66 g Carbohydrate (14 g Fibre, 50 g Sugar); 3 g Protein; 0 mg Sodium

   Consuming large quantities of fruit each day has been shown to slow and even prevent age-related macular (eye) degeneration.

Popeye Plus

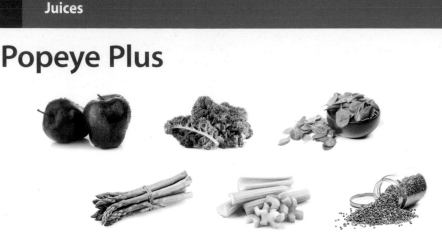

Spinach and hemp protein is a winning combination in this juice. While some juices have a cleansing nature and others are stimulating, this juice is building. Kale provides potassium and vitamin B6 to help support heart health. Celery brings great hydration with balanced electrolytes, and asparagus provides chromium, a trace mineral that expedites the transfer of glucose from the blood into cells. Although any apples can be used, ambrosia apples have a particularly strong nectar flavour, which can help offset any bitterness from the greens.

Medium ambrosia apples	2	2
Kale leaves	3	3
Baby spinach	1 cup	250 mL
Asparagus stalks	4	4
Celery stalks	4	4
Hemp protein powder	1 tbsp.	15 mL

Juice all the fruit and vegetables, then whisk in the hemp protein powder. Makes 1 serving.

1 serving: *310 Calories; 4 g Total Fat (0.5 g Mono, 1 g Poly, 0 g Sat); 0 mg Cholesterol; 72 g Carbohydrate (19 g Fibre, 43 g Sugar); 16 g Protein; 190 mg Sodium*

Hemp protein is rich in omega-3 and -6 fatty acids, both of which support heart health and lower blood pressure. Adding hemp protein increases satiety and helps prevent spikes in blood sugar by slowing digestion.

Sprout Power

   Sprouts offer an outstanding nutrient-to-calorie ratio, meaning that adding these superfoods to your juice dramatically increases the nutrition without bulking up the calories. Both pea and alfalfa sprouts offer vitamin K, necessary for healthy blood and for its ability to bind calcium in bones and tissue. Beets are high in folate, which is essential for the synthesis of DNA within cells. Glycine betaine, a phytochemical found only in the beetroot, lowers the risk of coronary heart disease and stroke.

Sprouts, pea or alfalfa	1 cup	250 mL
Beets with greens	2	2
(or use 4 to 6 Swiss chard leaves)		
Celery stalks	2	2
Medium apple	1	1
Lime, peeled	1	1

Juice all the ingredients and stir lightly. Makes 1 serving.

1 serving: 210 Calories; 0 g Total Fat (0 g Mono, 0 g Poly, 0 g Sat); 0 mg Cholesterol; 45 g Carbohydrate (8 g Fibre, 30 g Sugar); 5 g Protein; 220 mg Sodium

Swiss chard and beets are actually the same plant, but one variety is grown for its bulbous root (the beet) while the other is grown for its fleshier leaves.

Spicy Fiesta

Whereas most juices are either sweet from a high fruit content or bitter from a high leaf content, this is one of the rare juices that has a savoury taste, reminiscent of salsa. Chili peppers are extremely high in vitamin C, and the spiciness helps boost your metabolism. This juice is very hydrating, and the sea salt helps balance the electrolytes.

Tomatoes	3	3
Small chili pepper or jalapeño pepper, seeds and stem removed	1	1
Green onion	1	1
Sprigs of cilantro	6	6
Basil leaves	4	4
Lime, peeled	1/2	1/2
Red bell pepper, seeds and stem removed	1	1
Sea salt	1/4 tsp.	1 mL

Juice the first 7 ingredients and then whisk in the sea salt. Makes 1 serving.

1 serving: 90 Calories; 1 g Total Fat (0 g Mono, 0 g Poly, 0 g Sat); 0 mg Cholesterol; 27 g Carbohydrate (5 g Fibre, 17 g Sugar); 5 g Protein; 560 mg Sodium

All peppers belong to the genus *Capsicum*, and they are unique in producing a chemical called capsaicin. All peppers have capsaicin, and in large amounts it produces the familiar burning sensation. When trimming a chili pepper it is best to wear gloves; the capsaicin can linger on the skin and burn for some time.

Tropical Morning

Blood oranges taste as though nature made her own combination of orange and raspberry. The red colour comes from a pigment called anthocyanin, which is a powerful antioxidant. The mango and papaya in this juice provide a velvety texture and are rich in nutrients including B vitamins. Mangoes are also reputed to have strong anti-cancer benefits.

Cantaloupe pieces	1/2 cup	125 mL
Mango, pitted	1	1
Medium blood orange, peeled	1	1
Papaya, seeded	1	1
Kiwi fruit	1	1
Ginger root (1 inch, 2.5 cm, piece)	1	1

Juice all the ingredients and stir lightly. Makes 1 serving.

1 serving: 350 Calories; 3 g Total Fat (0.5 g Mono, 0.5 g Poly, 1 g Sat); 0 mg Cholesterol; 101 g Carbohydrate (10 g Fibre, 83 g Sugar); 6 g Protein; 30 mg Sodium

Some people are sensitive to the fuzzy skin of kiwis; it can cause irritation in the mouth. Most people, however, are unbothered by it. If the skin doesn't bother you, juice the kiwi unpeeled.

Hearty and Hale

One of the great superfoods that is nutritious in smoothies and juices is spirulina. Also known as blue-green algae, spirulina is rich in a variety of nutrients, including some that are in short supply in other foods. The rich green powder is also extremely high in protein, about 60 to 70 percent by weight. Recent intriguing studies are beginning to hint at spirulina's ability to combat cancer. With spirulina, broccoli and a good dose of ginseng, this juice is a powerful health-building elixir.

Carrots	2	2
Kiwi fruit	1	1
Broccoli florets	3	3
Baby spinach	2 cups	500 mL
Spirulina powder	1 tsp.	5 mL
Ground ginseng	1/2 tsp.	2 mL

Juice the carrots, kiwi, broccoli and spinach. The kiwi skin can be left on. Whisk in the spirulina and ginseng. Makes 1 serving.

1 serving: *200 Calories; 2 g Total Fat (0 g Mono, trace Poly, 0 g Sat); 0 mg Cholesterol; 57 g Carbohydrate (20 g Fibre, 20 g Sugar); 5 g Protein; 360 mg Sodium*

Ginseng contains a wide assortment of micronutrients, and it acts to reduce stress, regulate metabolism and increase energy levels.

Immunity Booster

The hint of curry in this juice comes from a small dose of turmeric. Turmeric reduces inflammation throughout many body systems. Chronic inflammation is one of the precursors to more serious diseases, so reducing it can prevent serious health problems. Mixing turmeric and tomatoes with fat increases the bioavailability of their nutrients, so we've added hemp powder, a good source of omega-3s and -6s, to help out.

Collard greens	1 cup	250 mL
Baby spinach	1 cup	250 mL
Medium green apples	2	2
Carrots	4	4
Tomato	1	1
Turmeric	1/2 tsp.	2 mL
Sea salt	1/4 tsp.	1 mL
Hemp protein powder	1 tsp.	5 mL

Juice the fruits and vegetables, then whisk in the turmeric, salt and hemp protein powder. Makes 1 serving.

1 serving: 290 Calories; 2.5 g Total Fat (1 g Mono, 0.5 g Poly, 0 g Sat); 0 mg Cholesterol; 81 g Carbohydrate (12 g Fibre, 47 g Sugar); 11 g Protein; 770 mg Sodium

The most active compound (health-wise) in turmeric is curcumin. This compound has powerful antioxidant and anti-inflammatory effects on the body. Furthermore, curcumin increases the activity of the body's own antioxidant enzymes.

Berry Smart

Berry lovers will delight in this delicious and richly coloured juice. Each of these fruits is high in antioxidants and other nutrients. Flavonoids called anthocyanidins are found almost exclusively in berries, and they can cross the blood-brain barrier into the learning and memory centres of the brain.

Studies have shown a reduction in metal decline in women who consume berries a couple of times a week. Matcha, or green tea powder, is finely ground, shade-grown tea that has a very high content of theanine and chlorophyll. Theanine improves mental focus.

Raspberries	1/2 cup	125 mL
Blackberries	1/2 cup	125 mL
Strawberries	1 cup	250 mL
Blueberries	1 cup	250 mL
Kiwi fruit	1	1
Matcha	1 tsp.	5 mL

Juice the first 5 ingredients, then lightly whisk in the matcha. Makes 1 serving.

1 serving: 180 Calories; 1.5 g Total Fat (0 g Mono, 0 g Poly, 0 g Sat); 0 mg Cholesterol; 57 g Carbohydrate (16 g Fibre, 35 g Sugar); 6 g Protein; 0 mg Sodium

Although from a culinary perspective the kiwi fruit doesn't seem like a berry, it is a true berry in the botanical sense. Ironically, strawberries, raspberries and blackberries aren't berries at all, but rather are aggregate fruits. The blueberry, aptly named in this case, is also a true berry.

Herbal Tonic

Herbs are often forgotten about as promoters of good health because we use them in such small quantities. Nevertheless, several common garden herbs are excellent additions to juices because of their rich vitamin and mineral content. Rosemary has compounds that benefit the brain and a unique compound called carnosic acid that significantly enhances eye health. The chili pepper provides both flavour and a big dose of vitamin C, as well as a good boost to the metabolism.

Medium apples	2	2
Carrots	4	4
Beet	1	1
Sprigs of parsley	4	4
Sprigs of fresh thyme	7	7
Sprig of fresh rosemary	1	1
Small chili pepper, seeds and stem removed	1	1

Juice all the ingredients and stir lightly. Makes 1 serving.

1 serving: 260 Calories; 1 g Total Fat (0 g Mono, 0 g Poly, 0 g Sat); 0 mg Cholesterol; 78 g Carbohydrate (19 g Fibre, 50 g Sugar); 5 g Protein; 240 mg Sodium

Parsley can promote muscle contractions, so pregnant women should avoid this herb.

INDEX